IMPROVING THE PRIMARY SCHOOL

The aim of raising standards is a familiar theme to anyone currently working in education. In this short and practical book, the latest research is used to inform the advice given by an educationalist who has a proven track record at the chalk face. Joan Dean gives wise direction to those in leadership positions. The book:

- reviews the current trends and developments in education;
- summarises the latest thinking and translates it into practice;
- remains optimistic, energetic *and* realistic about what can be achieved in school.

Issues covered include:

- the school development plan;
- classroom practice and organisation;
- professional development of teachers;
- the roles of parents and governors.

Joan Dean has been a headteacher, senior primary adviser and chief inspector during her years in education. She was awarded an OBE for services to education in 1980. She has published widely in the field and is the author of three other titles for Routledge.

EDUCATIONAL MANAGEMENT SERIES

Series editor: Cyril Poster

IMPROVING THE PRIMARY SCHOOL

Joan Dean

London and New York

First published 1999
by Routledge
11 New Fetter Lane, London EC4P 4EE

Simultaneously published in the USA and Canada
by Routledge
29 West 35th Street, New York, NY 10001

© 1999 Joan Dean

Typeset in Garamond by
M Rules
Printed and bound in Great Britain by
Page Bros (Norwich) Ltd

British Library Cataloguing in Publication Data
A catalogue record for this book is available from the British Library

Library of Congress Cataloguing in Publication Data
Dean, Joan.
Improving the primary school / Joan Dean.
p. cm. – (Educational management series)
Includes bibliographical references (p.   ) and index.
1. Elementary school administration – Great Britain.
2. School improvement programmes – Great Britain.
I. Title.   II. Series.
LB2822.5.D394   1999
372.12′00941–dc21   98-24878

ISBN 0–415–16895–3

CONTENTS

1

INTRODUCTION

Sue Jamieson took over Little Manor Primary School as headteacher from a head who had been there for thirty years and who had mentally retired some years before he physically left. The five teachers in the school had largely gone their own ways, making what they could of the National Curriculum, and it was thanks to the governors rather than the head that the school had remained solvent.

Parents had been kept at arm's length. The school made no attempt to explain its work to them. There was no parent–teacher association and there were few opportunities for teachers and parents to meet and talk. The annual parents' meeting was poorly attended and generally was used by parents as an opportunity to air criticisms of the school. As a result of the lack of contact and general dissatisfaction, a number of children drifted away to the school in the next village if parents could manage to transport them there.

Sue started by arranging to talk with each of the five teachers individually, with the idea of finding out what they thought about their work, the kinds of values which guided them and their receptiveness to the idea of working together. Like any group of people, their views varied, but they were at one in their devotion to the children and were conscious that their work lacked continuity because they had had so little discussion as a staff. The National Curriculum had helped to some extent but they thought it would be useful to come together to discuss some of their work.

They were very varied in their approaches to teaching. Janet, who taught the youngest class, was very informal, whereas John, who taught Years 5 and 6, was more concerned about preparing his children for the secondary school and did a good deal of class teaching in spite of the fact that his class contained two age groups. The other members of staff used a mixture of methods, with more formal approaches tending to dominate.

The school development plan had in the past been entirely the creation of the headteacher, with very little discussion about it with teachers or with governors. It was, in any case, a very limited document which did little to move the school forward.

There had also been no attempt previously to appoint people as coordinators and very little emphasis on staff development, though everyone had been to some courses in preparation for the introduction of the National Curriculum. Closure days for staff development tended to be used for sorting out materials and preparing work.

The governors of the school were a good group, well aware of what had happened to the school under the previous head, and they were hoping when they appointed Sue to see something of a transformation.

Sue started by setting aside a Saturday for staff and governors to discuss where they thought the school was going and their visions of the future. She got someone from the local authority to introduce the day by talking about current research on effective schools and teachers, and he went on to suggest that the staff should try to envisage their ideal school of three years' time. They worked in small groups of governors and staff to set this down and then shared all the views. In the afternoon there was a discussion on the values they held and their implications.

Sue took away all the material they had produced, grouping similar statements and wording them in a similar way. She then took them back to the staff. Between them they condensed the lists and reworded some of the points to make them more comprehensive. Eventually they had a school statement of vision and values which they took back to the governors, who made further suggestions. This was further refined into a statement of the school's mission which was just one sentence summing up the most important aspects of the vision and value statements.

The next task was to consider the implications of each of these statements: this involved a series of meetings between staff and those governors who happened to be free. This work informed the next development plan which was carefully set out with clear statements of aims and objectives, timing, costing and success criteria, each related in some way to the statements of vision. An important item was the introduction of curriculum coordinators. As there was a shortage of coordinators, some people had to take on two roles and everyone had to do something. The group also managed to link up with two other small primary schools and share some expertise. The staff welcomed this in principle, but were hesitant about the implication that a colleague might want to see them teach. They also had doubts about how much was involved as they worked out what the responsibilities of these posts might be. This work started a new interest in staff development in that everyone realised that he or she would need to go to some courses if the job were to be done thoroughly. Sue set aside most of the training money for this purpose.

The staff gradually worked together to develop policies for many aspects of the work of the school. They developed a record-keeping system which reflected clearly the development and progress of individual children and agreed that they would use this as children moved from class to class. They spent time discussing the problem of teaching classes that covered two age groups, and undertook some action research to see whether they could find better ways of teaching particular topics. They also spent time evaluating the changes they were making.

None of this was easy. Sue was asking teachers to change their culture from one where they had been autonomous and independent in their own classrooms to one where they shared ideas, planned together and saw one another teach. People grumbled about the meetings but nevertheless came to them and contributed. Some teachers felt that they were being asked to make decisions which the head ought to make – 'After all, she's paid to make the decisions!' Others welcomed the opportunity to be involved and eventually everyone came to expect involvement.

Gradually the school developed. The results of the Standard Assessment Tasks improved year by year and parents stopped looking for schools elsewhere. Teachers felt themselves to be part of a team and brought their problems and difficulties as well as their successes to colleagues so that they might help each other. Four years after Sue came to the school, there was an inspection and a very good report.

An important element in this development was Sue's constant interest in what was happening in the classrooms. She visited her colleagues regularly and held many discussions with individuals and groups about the best way to teach different topics and children. She did a good deal of teaching herself, working alongside colleagues and planning with them, showing by example what could be done, but in a non-threatening way with the other teachers fully involved. She gradually harnessed parental support and introduced the idea of parents helping in the classrooms, where they were made to feel welcome and so gave their full support. There was also a programme of paired reading involving the parents.

Perhaps the most important factors in the gradual improvement in work of the school were Sue's warmth, tact and ability to persuade people to help fulfil the vision they had planned. She also generated an atmosphere of trust. People knew where they stood with her and appreciated her encouragement in their work. She delegated a good deal and colleagues felt that they were trusted but supported in carrying out the work they had agreed to undertake.

This is an example of a headteacher who did many of the things which research suggests are characteristic of effective schools and in this case she was successful. We know a good deal about effective schools but are still learning both about effectiveness and how to improve schools which are not effective. This is partly because while it is generally understood that certain characteristics are related to school effectiveness, it is less well known that they are causal. Sammons *et al.* (1995 : 2) state:

> It is important to recognise that school effectiveness research results do not provide a blue-print or recipe for the creation of more effective schools. . . . School improvement efforts require a particular focus on

the process of change and understanding of the history and context of the specific institutions. . . . The findings should not . . . be applied mechanically and without reference to a school's particular context. Rather they can be seen as a helpful starting point for school self-evaluation and review.

What we do know is that improving a school may require teachers to change values and attitudes and this is extremely difficult.

What is an effective school? Different researches have taken different criteria and it is important to consider these in assessing the implications of any piece of research. Sammons *et al.* (1995 : 3) define an effective school as one 'in which pupils progress further than might be expected from consideration of the intake'. Beare *et al.* (1989 : 13) suggest that being effective 'assumes achieving better results with resources you already have'. Stoll and Fink (1996) identify four characteristics of effectiveness. They say:

We choose to define a school as effective if it:

- promotes progress for *all* its pupils beyond what would be expected given consideration of initial attainment and background factors;
- ensures that each pupil achieves the highest standard possible;
- enhances aspects of pupil achievement and development;
- continues to improve from year to year.

(Stoll and Fink 1996 : 28)

They also add 'the world of work now looks for young people who demonstrate flexibility, creativity and problem-solving skills and who are able to cooperate in the workplace' (p.28). It would be easy to forget the importance of skills of this kind in attempting to meet the current concerns about numeracy and literacy. They were skills which the 'trendy' schools of the sixties and seventies considered important and we need to continue to train them. One way of judging the effectiveness of education would be to consider how far a young person leaving school is able to learn without a teacher. Good primary schools start children along this road.

Coleman *et al.* (1966) and Jencks *et al.* (1972) concluded from studies of schools in the United States that school achievement was largely determined by a child's family background and that school could make comparatively little difference. Later research is less pessimistic. Rutter *et al.* (1979), Mortimore *et* al. (1988) and others have shown that schools do make a difference. Schools with very similar intake vary considerably in what their pupils achieve. Reynolds and Cuttance (1992) suggest that the difference is between 8 and 15 per cent. Scheerens (1992) suggests that in extreme cases the difference can be as much as a year between pupils of similar ability and background in different schools.

Many writers give lists of the characteristics of effective schools and class-rooms (e.g. Beare *et al.* (1989), Edmonds (1979), Purkey and Smith (1985), Scheerens (1992), Sammons *et al.* (1995)). The following are included in various lists:

- There is strong leadership from the headteacher who has a vision of what the school could be like, shares this widely and encourages others to contribute.
- All members of staff are committed to a shared vision for the whole school.
- The headteacher and other senior members of staff lead in emphasising learning.
- Children's learning is at the core of all that the school does.
- The school climate is conditioned by high expectations about learning.
- There are clear goals which are commonly agreed.
- Decision making is a democratic process.
- There is trust among the staff and between the staff and headteacher, and teachers are not hesitant about consulting colleagues over problems.
- Achievement is characteristic of the whole school and is high year after year.
- There is order and discipline in the school.
- There is purposeful teaching and positive reinforcement for good work and behaviour.
- Pupils are given responsibility and self-esteem is fostered.
- Staff development is seen as important by all members of staff.
- There is systematic evaluation of all aspects of the work of the school.
- The environment has been made attractive and convenient for the work to be done.
- Parents are involved in the school and support its work.
- Governors have a clear idea of their role and that of the headteacher, and support the work of the school.

There are also many research findings about effective teachers. These include the following:

- Effective teachers prepare well and have clear goals for their teaching.
- They aim to make as much teaching contact with all their children as possible.
- They aim to see that children spend as much time profitably on-task as possible.
- They have high expectations for all children.
- They make clear presentations which match the level of the children.
- They structure work well and tell children the purpose of the work they are doing and the targets they hope the children will achieve.

- They are flexible in varying teaching behaviour and activities.
- They use many higher-order questions which demand thinking on the part of the children.
- They give frequent feedback to children about how they are doing.
- They make appropriate and frequent use of praise for both achievement and behaviour.
- They keep good records of the attainment and progress of individual children and these are shared and used. Progress in learning is constantly assessed.
- Their classrooms are well organised, ordered and attractive.
- They reflect on the work they and the children have done and evaluate progress towards goals.

Research also finds that too much negative criticism has a negative effect on achievement.

Reynolds and Cuttance (1992) make the point that schools have different effects on different children and different groups of children. It is also obvious that there will be variance in effectiveness according to the teacher. Research suggests that schools need both support and pressure (Fullan 1992).

Ofsted (1997) has studied schools which were failing and which have improved. Those which have improved most rapidly have:

- Strong leadership by the headteacher.
- Effective management by senior staff.
- Clear action plans with specific and measurable targets and outcomes.
- Committed teachers intent on improving matters.
- Good communication between the school and parents.
- Tackled poor behaviour and attendance satisfactorily.
- Developed plans for the National Curriculum and schemes of work for subjects.
- Effective financial management.

(Ofsted 1997 : 10)

There has recently been comment that teachers in primary schools are paying insufficient attention to the basic skills. The evidence from research (e.g. Bassey (1978), DES (1978, 1985a), Galton and Simon (1980), Galton *et al.* (1980), Neville Bennett *et al.* (1984), Mortimore *et al.* (1988), Tizard *et al.* (1988), Galton and Patrick (1990), Campbell and Neill (1994), Webb and Vulliamy (1996)) is that teachers have always paid a great deal of attention to basic skills, and before the advent of the National Curriculum may have neglected other aspects of education as a result. What is also clear, however, is that time spent on basic skill work is not always well spent. For example, Neville Bennett *et al.* (1984) found that teachers failed to match work to children in a substantial number of cases. They were concerned about matching work where the less able were concerned but had a blind spot for the more able, who frequently had work which was too easy for them.

Schools are currently working in a difficult climate. The costs of many public services have risen and are outstripping revenue so that schools are suffering from many shortages. They are being placed in a market situation where they are expected to treat parents, and to some extent children, as customers and to satisfy their requirements. They are also in competition with each other for pupils. They are being held accountable to a much greater extent than formerly, and this, allied with the need for teachers to work together more than in the past, means that the classroom teacher in the primary school has less autonomy in some senses. However, Alexander (1984 : 172) gives a definition of autonomy which still holds good for the individual teacher and school:

This autonomy . . . is a commitment to rationality; a preparedness always to question 'authoritative' pronouncements, never to accept them at face value; a search for intellectual independence through an awareness of and an ability to examine alternative propositions; yet at the same time a consciousness that knowledge itself is provisional, modifiable and cumulative, so that 'knowing' itself is also an aspiration rather than an achievement.

This outlook is important at the present time when teachers are being presented with many ideas and suggestions, all of which need to be examined carefully rather than taken at face value. Webb and Vulliamy (1996) studied a group of fifty schools recommended by their LEAs as having good practice and looked at the changes that had taken place in them. They found that:

These changes – in relation to governors, local management of schools (LMS), parents as consumers and the introduction of quality assurance mechanisms – were found to be both transforming teachers' work and having a fundamental impact on the culture of primary schools.
(Webb and Vulliamy 1996 : 8)

Creemers (1994 : 11) suggests that 'One of the most important goals of educational policy is undoubtedly to create a solution for the problem of educational inequality with regard to the socioeconomic background of pupils and schools.' This is a problem which we have to solve. Schools serving disadvantaged areas vary considerably in what they achieve. We need all schools in such areas to rise to the level of the best.

There is also a need in all western countries to educate the whole population to a higher standard than ever before, since there are no longer many unskilled jobs and schools are expected to play their part in preparing young people for employment in a world where there is intense international competition for trade. New technology has transformed most industries and is in the process of transforming schools. We have hardly begun to explore the possibilities of new technology.

We also need to educate young people to live in a rapidly shrinking world where what happens in one country affects many others, where societies are increasingly pluralistic. We are also using up the earth's resources and damaging our environment to an alarming extent: the next generation will have to live with this and must be educated about it.

All of this suggests that we need to help our children to achieve more than the children have done in the past. This is not to suggest that teachers have failed in their work previously. Primary schools all over the country have produced some outstanding work over the years. The problem is that not enough schools produce exemplary work and the demands for educated people are higher than ever before. While education has done reasonably well with the average child, there is a long tail of children who are not achieving and many HMI reports testify to the fact that some schools are not extending the most able children.

This book sets out to offer suggestions to schools about how they can improve their work. There has been a good deal of work compiled on school improvement. The International School Improvement Project (ISIP), which involves fourteen countries, defines improvement as 'a systematic, sustained effort aimed at change in learning conditions and other related internal conditions in one or more schools, with the ultimate aim of accomplishing educational goals more effectively' (Van Velsen *et al.* 1985 : 48).

Ofsted (1994a : 6) defines improvement as ways in which schools:

- raise standards;
- enhance quality;
- increase efficiency;
- achieve greater success in promoting pupils' spiritual, moral, social and cultural development, in a word, the ethos of the school.

Stoll and Fink (1996 : 43) define school improvement as a series of concurrent and recurring processes in which a school:

- enhances pupil outcomes;
- focuses on teaching and learning;
- builds the capacity to take charge of change regardless of its source;
- defines its own direction;
- assesses the current culture and works to develop positive cultural norms;
- has strategies to achieve its goals;
- addresses the internal conditions that enhance change;

- maintains momentum during periods of turbulence;
- monitors and evaluates its process, progress, achievement and development.

The DfEE Standards and Effectiveness Unit is reported in Croner's School Governors' Briefing (January 1998) as recommending a five-stage cycle of school improvement. This follows the cycle of:

- analysis – looking critically at pupils' current achievement;
- bench-marking – comparing this with the performance of schools with similar intakes;
- target-setting – setting realistic but challenging targets;
- action to improve performance – this may involve changing the ways pupils are grouped, the style of teaching and learning, the way homework is set and marked or the way parents are involved in their children's education;
- review of achievements – the school evaluates how well it has done against its targets and compares its performance against national data. The whole process then starts again.

Many factors are bringing about change in schools. Those establishments which are working well may feel that the suggestion that change is needed implies that there is something wrong with what they are doing already. This is not the case. No organisation stands still. It must either improve or decline. There is always scope for improvement in some aspect of the life and work of a school since children can always be encouraged to do better and teachers are continually finding better ways of working. All improvement involves change. In any case schools have had to deal with unprecedented amounts of externally imposed change in the last few years and demands for change are likely to continue.

We have already noted that schools are preparing children for a changing world. The skills and knowledge that were appropriate yesterday may not be appropriate in tomorrow's world. Stoll and Fink (1996 : 120) quote Reich who

contends that people who will succeed in a post modern world would possess the following four sets of basic skills:

- abstraction, the capacity for discovering patterns and meaning;
- systems thinking, to see relationships among phenomena;
- experimentation, the ability to see one's own way through continuous thinking;
- the social skills to collaborate with others.

They also quote the Conference Board [of Canada] which:

expands the conventional basics to include critical thinking, problem solving and technological literacy. The list also includes personal management skills like positive attitude, responsibility and adapt-ability. The skills list adds a set of teamwork skills which include the ability to contribute to organisational goals.

(Stoll and Fink 1996 : 121)

A school cannot stand still in today's world. We are living through a period of change which affects us all and schools are part of this. We need the flexibil-ity and the courage to meet the changes that are happening around us.

2

ASSESSING RESEARCH

There are a number of issues which should be borne in mind in considering research into school effectiveness. There are now many studies of effective schools but some have greater validity than others and anyone reading the research needs to ask questions of the text:

1   *What sample has been chosen? How large is it? Does it include different types and sizes of schools? What age groups does it deal with? What generalisations can be made from it?*

Many of the samples used are schools in disadvantaged areas, partly because these schools give more cause for concern than schools in areas where children have many advantages. We know less about effectiveness in advantaged areas. We can also learn from samples in other countries but the differences in culture need to be taken into account.

2   *What criteria of effectiveness have been chosen?*

Many studies use children's performance in basic skills rather than the whole curriculum and these may be lower-order skills rather than those requiring creativity and higher-order thinking. Some have also been concerned with affective and social development and matters such as children's self-esteem and self-confidence. Reynolds and Cuttance (1992) point out that using lower-order skills as criteria may lead to passive types of learning being seen as more effective.

It is important that a range of criteria is used. For example, Rutter *et al.* (1979) used examination results, attendance, behaviour and delinquency in their study of secondary schools. Mortimore *et al.* (1988) used reading, mathematics (written), mathematics (practical), writing, speaking, attendance, behaviour and a range of attitudes. They also used measures such as the socioeconomic status of the parents. In general the criteria used in most studies of school effectiveness tend to be more on the cognitive side than the non-cognitive.

3   *What measures of children's background have been included?*

Much of the work on effectiveness involves concern about the fact that schools do not start equal and the children's background is therefore important. The measures of background need to be sufficient to give a clear view of socioeconomic status and ethnic origin. Reynolds and Reid (1985 : 195) sum this up as follows: 'Outcomes cannot merely be seen as being produced by effective or ineffective schools without an assessment of which pupils, from which families and for which communities they are held to be effective or ineffective.'

4 *What is the time element in the study?*

Some studies are simply measures at one point in time. Others look at progress over a period. It is not enough to obtain good results for one year: good results over a long period are important. It also has to be recognised that year groups vary and a good year may be followed by a poor year.

Some researches are concerned with progress as well as achievement – for example, Mortimore *et al.* (1988). This gives a different point of view and is probably a better measure of the school's work than achievement alone. The introduction of baseline testing and the comparison of children's performance at different stages in schooling make the emphasis on progress more evident.

5 *What research techniques have been employed?*

In addition to statistical information already obtainable in the school, such as attendance figures, studies may include observation of classroom and management practice, examination of children's work, testing of various kinds, questionnaires to teachers, children and parents, interviews with teachers, children and parents, studies of the use of time, home visiting, action research with and by teachers, case studies and any other ideas the researchers can think of. It is important that more than one method is used so that information from one research activity is reinforced by another. For example, studies which rely entirely on questionnaires may unintentionally fail to ask important questions and those responding may fail to give important information. Questionnaires need to be backed up with other methods.

It is also important that the findings are valid and reliable. Validity is the extent to which a test or observations measure what they are intended to measure. Reliability is the extent to which the same results will be obtained if the measure is repeated.

6 *What methods of analysis have been used?*

The methods of analysis should make it possible to provide information about the ways that measures are related. However, it is important not to assume that when two measures are highly correlated one is the cause of the other. For example, many studies show that teacher expectation is an important element in children's achievement (e.g. Mortimore *et al.* (1988)). The obvious explanation is that the teacher's expectation causes the high achievement. But it could be that the children achieve well, making the teacher have high expectations of them, which in turn leads the teacher to make considerable demands upon them, which helps them to achieve more.

Most modern research uses highly sophisticated statistical techniques which allow different factors to be isolated.

Different researches tend to come up with slightly different results that are affected by the way they are analysed. But we are concerned here with the results which come from a number of studies that confirm each other. Macbeth (1994 : 308) suggests that there are three questions which should be applied to research findings:

1   Do several studies draw the same conclusions?
2   Is there a relative dearth of contrary evidence?
3   Do the findings accord with common sense and the experience of teachers?

Some research suggests that schools have different effects on different pupils. This is one reason why it is important for researches to be carried out in affluent as well as disadvantaged areas. Nuttall *et al.* (1989), for example, found differences with respect to gender and ethnic background. They also found that some schools narrowed the gap between the most and least able while others widened it. Mortimore *et al.* (1988), on the other hand, found that schools which did well by boys also did well by girls. It is reasonable to assume that schools are not uniformly effective across different areas of curriculum since these reflect differences in teaching ability. A primary school may be more effective with some age groups than others according to the teachers concerned. Cuttance (1985 : 18) suggests that 'Positive effects at one level may be offset by negative effects at other levels, therefore the net effect when the organisational structure is left out of the model is to find only small school effects, particularly when the average performance across all levels within school is employed as the measure of outcomes.'

Ouston and Maughan (1985 : 32) note that 'The notion of common, easily measured, generally accepted, educational outcome measures appropriate to all children clearly does not reflect the real work of schools.' They also note the importance of the hidden curriculum, 'the assumptions, values, attitudes and behaviour of pupils and teachers which are not in evidence in the formal curriculum. These are, almost by definition, difficult to measure, yet they seem likely to play a major part in explaining why some schools are more successful than others' (p.33).

Education, like other aspects of our world, is not stagnant. The possibilities of new technology may make tomorrow's schools almost unrecognisable and they may need different qualities from those which research shows to be effective at present.

3

THE SCHOOL CULTURE

Vision and values

Many writers and researchers stress the importance of shared vision in schools (e.g. Bennis and Nanus (1985), Beare *et al.* (1989), Riddell and Brown (1991), Murgatroyd and Morgan (1992), Whitaker (1993), Sammons *et al.* (1995)). Murgatroyd and Morgan (1992 : 81) suggest that a school vision 'should be defined as a vivid picture of a challenging yet desirable future state that strongly meets the needs of the students and is widely seen as a significant improvement on the current state'. They go on to say:

> Everyone involved in the school . . . should be encouraged to articulate the meaning of the vision for them personally once it has been developed. The vision should become a basis for encouraging, enabling, empowering and developing the staff of the school, and should be regarded as the cornerstone for all the actions of the school.
> (Murgatroyd and Morgan 1992 : 83)

Clegg and Billington (1997 : 66) suggest

> that a vision for a school should encompass broad agreement about the following:
> - the nature and purpose of education;
> - the nature of the school's curriculum;
> - the working relationships within school;
> - the way the school relates to its community.

This leaves the school with the question of how to set about the task of creating and implementing a vision of this kind. Most headteachers have a vision in their own minds of how they see the school developing, but this vision needs not only to be widely shared but developed and owned by the staff and governors as a group. The description in Chapter 1 of how a headteacher worked to change a school suggested that staff and governors met for a day,

14

preferably a Saturday so that all the governors could be present, to try to articulate a vision for the school. Small groups of staff and governors might brainstorm their ideas about how they would like the school to be in, say, three years' time. Their statements could be recorded on large sheets of paper and posted around the room. Their findings can then be arranged under various headings, such as Curriculum, Personal and Social Education, Behaviour, Parent Relationships, Teaching Methods, Staff Development, and so on.

The next task is to try to sum up each group of statements in one sentence so that there is a simple vision statement of one short paragraph. This may be best done by one or two people rather than the whole group. The statements then become the overall goals for the school which should be reflected in the school development plan. It is important that the vision agreed should be achievable and possible within the resources available to the school. The ideas expressed in the vision statements can be further summarised to provide a one-sentence mission statement of what the school is about. This can be used frequently so that everyone concerned becomes familiar with it.

Further work is then needed to make the vision part of everyone's thinking. One useful activity is to take each statement and, working in pairs or small groups, generate statements about what each means in practical terms.

Older children can also have some involvement in the vision statement if it contains major goals for the school. The goals also need to be shared with parents.

This work will undoubtedly bring to the fore people's values in education and may give rise to conflict as to what is important. However, if the school is to develop, such conflict needs to be worked through and people need to accept that some of the statements will reflect values that are different from their own. It can be useful to follow up the vision statement with an attempt to state a set of values for the school.

Clegg and Billington (1997 : 44) make the following points about values:

> What we can confirm is that running a school is fundamentally con-
> cerned with values and beliefs and, while structures and systems have
> a part to play in school organisation, they only represent values and
> beliefs, and further, the way people behave within these structures is
> a basic manifestation of the school culture.

School culture and collegiality

Every organisation has its own culture – a sense of 'this is the way we do things here'. Alexander (1984 : 156) notes the difference between ideology and culture:

> *Ideology* is the collection of ideas, values and beliefs which explain and
> legitimise the activities and situation of particular social groups.

Culture encompasses both ideology and the social and material structures in which it is embedded, with their attendant behaviour patterns and networks of relationships.

Delamont (1987) and Pollard (1985) refer to culture as 'institutional bias'. Delamont describes it as follows:

> The concept of institutional bias draws attention to tacit understandings about behaviour, values and practices which, though produced through past activity, may be experienced in the present as part of the existing social context of an organisation such as a school.
>
> (Delamont 1987 : 107)

Beare *et al.* (1989 : 173) list the following aspects of a school culture:

- the underlying philosophy and/or ideology espoused by the leaders and members;
- the ways in which that philosophy is translated into an operational mission or purpose;
- the respective value sets of leaders and others (both within the organisation and those directly affected by its operation);
- the quality (as well as the nature) of personal and interpersonal actions and interactions;
- the metaphors which consciously or unconsciously serve as frameworks for thinking and action;
- the sagas, myths, stories and folk heroes and celebrations which serve to generate or bolster incentive and motivation;
- the many other tangible and intangible manifestations which hitherto have been given scant importance but have potential and power in the organisation.

Nias *et al.* (1989 : 32–3) describe the factors which they found in the schools they studied which helped to create the culture:

> The same range of factors seemed to be significant in all the schools, unique though each one was. These were: the school buildings and organisational arrangements, the people who worked there, their histories and that of the school. Each of these affected the school's culture, first by determining the nature and extent of interaction between staff members, and second by helping to decide who among them had authority and influence. . . .
>
> Interaction was influenced by institutional and personal factors within each school. . . . Buildings and organisational arrangements affected interaction by controlling individual opportunities for inter-

action, whereas personal histories, particularly past experiences in the school, affected personal inclination to interact.

Expectation is an important factor in schools. The headteacher's expectation of teachers influences their work and in turn their expectation of children in the classroom influences the children's performance. Headteachers need to work to raise teachers' expectations so that demands are made of all children. Classroom teachers need to create a climate in which children are expected to work hard and achieve.

Mortimore *et al.* (1988 : 285) found that expectation was an important element in school culture:

> Where the head, by example, has high expectation and sets a tone which is positive about learning and positive about pupils, it is much more likely that teachers and, indeed, pupils will also exhibit such traits. If the school is positive, and has an atmosphere in which it is expected that all pupils will succeed (even if not at the same level or at the same time), then pupils will feel valued; so will staff.

A school with a strong culture may also find that there is a counter-culture developing and this can be confusing. Different groups within a large school may have different beliefs and norms and some of these may conflict. A headteacher has to work to bring people together as far as possible, allowing for the fact that people will have different values which affect the way they work.

Teachers may react to a developing culture or institutional bias in many ways. Delamont (1987) lists four possible reactions:

- acceptance – this could be agreement or the line of least resistance;
- bypassing – 'a withdrawal from the institutional bias behind the defence of autonomy, expertise or both' (p.114). The teacher just gets on with his or her own way of doing things in the classroom;
- subversion – the teacher creates a degree of personal power and influence and may change the institutional bias;
- challenge – the teacher feels a real sense of having to fight the school ethos in order to achieve his or her pedagogic ends.

Delamont also notes that 'staff room culture is an important influence on any individual teacher's work experience' (p.118).

Purkey and Smith (1985 : 356) note that culture strongly affects the academic performance of children.

> The most persuasive research suggests that student academic performance is strongly affected by school culture. This culture is composed of values, norms and roles existing within institutionally distinct

structures of governance, communication, educational practice and policies and so on. Successful schools are found to have a culture that produces a climate or 'ethos' conducive to learning and teaching.

MacGilchrist *et al.* (1995) identify three dimensions to school culture:

- *Professional relationships* The relationships to each other held by pupils, support staff, governors, parents and external agencies as well as the head-teacher and teachers; the quality of leadership and extent of shared leadership; the degree of collegiality and openness; teamwork; the balance of independence and interdependence.
- *Organisational arrangements* The management of the school's structures, systems and environment; roles and responsibilities; decision-making systems; communication; pupils' grouping; pastoral care; discipline; rewards.
- *Opportunities for learning* 'The extent to which there is a focus on learning for both pupils and adults and the nature of that focus are a key factor' (p.41); the curriculum on offer; equal opportunities; special needs provision; professional development opportunities for teachers.

The headteacher is very important in creating and developing the school culture. Every headteacher needs to consider what he or she wants the school culture to be and then how best it can be developed.

Headteachers influence the culture by many of their actions, by what they select for praise and encouragement, by what they reward, by the decisions they make, by the material they select for assemblies, by their relationships, by the way they deal with the school's finances, by the encouragement they give to collaborative work by teachers, by the organisation of their rooms, and so on. Culture is also supported by the way the school selects 'heroes' – people who are examples of the values and vision – to tell the children about. Celebrations also exemplify culture. Almost everything a headteacher does affects the school climate.

Nias *et al.* (1989 : 34) found that in their study of primary schools, 'heads exercised a particularly powerful control on staff interaction. By coordinating staffs' work themselves, or by encouraging staff to plan and work together, heads increased or restricted staff interaction.'

They also found that assemblies were important:

> The fact of assembly symbolised the existence of a school and therefore of a school culture, every stage of a particular assembly was replete with symbolic implication. Specific aspects of the way assemblies were conducted emphasised their ritual importance, indicated assumptions about relationships or taught attitudes and values, both implicitly and explicitly.
>
> (Nias *et al.* 1989 : 42)

In considering culture, thought should be given to the culture of the children. Teachers in secondary schools are tending to find that there is a strong anti-academic culture among all young people and among boys in particular. It is not 'cool' to work hard. This is also evident among some older primary school children and a school needs to bear this in mind in considering the school culture.

Children will also have their own view of the school culture which will be different from that of the teachers. In assessing culture it is important to ask children what they think. Schools also need to consider how they socialise children into the school culture. Assemblies play an important role here, but the example of teachers, the way children are treated by teachers and the way they are encouraged to treat each other are all elements of involving children in the school culture. Parents are also involved. An aspect of the school culture is a view of the part parents can be expected to play in the education of their children.

There is evidence (Sammons *et al.* (1995) and many others) that giving pupils responsibility makes for a more effective school. This helps to raise self-esteem in the pupils and 'there can be quite a substantial gain in effectiveness when the self-esteem of pupils is raised, when they have an active role in the life of the school, and when they are given responsibility for their own learning' (p.21).

It is also necessary to consider how teachers coming new to the school and particularly newly qualified teachers will be socialised into the school culture. The head and governors will almost certainly have had this at the back of their minds when making the appointment, since the usually unspoken question 'Will this person fit in?' is one which people naturally consider in making an appointment. But thought needs to be given after the appointment about the ways in which the new teacher becomes acquainted with the school climate and ways of doing things. This is partly the role of a mentor in the case of the newly qualified teacher and for all new teachers there should be formal opportunities to learn about how things are done in the school. All new teachers need induction. Teddlie (1994), in reporting a study of schools in Louisiana, notes that the more effective schools had a consistency in teaching methods throughout the school. This is more likely when teachers feel themselves to be part of a similar culture. It will arise naturally if teachers are encouraged to discuss the way they teach and observe each other at work.

What sort of climate creates an effective school? The point has already been made that teaching and learning should be given a high priority. There is also evidence (e.g. Campbell (1988), Scheerens (1992), Webb and Vulliamy (1996)) that effective schools involve staff in the decision-making process and there is collegiality in the sense that teachers support each other, offer each other help and criticism, see themselves working in a common enterprise with common goals. Campbell (1988 : 287–8) describes this state of things as follows:

The teachers exist in a school in which constructive and critical scrutiny of each other's practice is the normal expectation, INSET is seen as valuable for the school and people feed back what seems useful. . . . The teachers committed to collegiality see the atmosphere of the school as the element most critical to its maintenance and derive strong personal and professional satisfaction from their involvement in, and contribution to, its continuance.

Clegg and Billington (1997 : 41) note that :

The most productive relationships appear to be those which offer genuine collaboration between teachers rather than a forced collegiality. This means teachers working together because they want to and deriving real benefit from planning together, observing each other and assisting each other in reflection about their work.

D. Hargreaves and Hopkins (1993) make the point that many attempts at school improvement fail if they do not take account of the school culture. Effective change may require a change in the culture of the school. This takes time and can appear threatening.

Teachers in primary schools have tended to work in isolation, each in their own classroom. They have valued their autonomy and were often worried when someone came to observe what they were doing. The National Curriculum has gone some way to changing this in that more schools do a certain amount of specialist teaching, especially where older children are concerned, and there is now a need for coordination which has brought teachers together to discuss how best to achieve it.

It is now necessary to go further and work together on many aspects of the life of the school to achieve what has come to be called collegiality. The staff of a primary school needs to be a team. Dyer (1987) lists the following characteristics of an effective team.

- The ability to make sound, free and informed choices or decisions.
- A clear understanding and acceptance of the goals (targets) by all team members.
- A climate of trust and support.
- The ability to identify and work through differences between people rather than the willingness to ignore or suppress them.
- An understanding by team members of their roles and how they fit into the overall framework of both the team and the organisation.

The staff of a school is not only a group of teachers. In many schools now there are various kinds of support assistants. These need to be part of the culture. Clegg and Billington (1997 : 96) suggest the following as rights of support staff:

- to be regarded as colleagues who have a full part to play in the school;
- to be included in discussion about whole school issues and in particular to be consulted about aspects which impact upon their specific areas;
- to have access to staff development opportunities;
- to have some input into the planning and assessing of curriculum provision.

They go on to say, 'It is a responsibility of the class teacher to involve the assistant fully in what is happening. . . . This involves class teachers spending time explaining the learning intentions behind activities and providing guidance to assistants about what strategies could be used to achieve these intentions' (p.96).

A. Hargreaves (1994) makes a distinction between 'contrived' collegiality and collaborative cultures. Contrived collegiality 'replaces spontaneous, unpredictable and difficult-to-control forms of teacher generated collaboration with forms of collaboration that are captured, contained and contrived by administrators instead' (p.196). He suggests that such collegiality can be cosmetic only and lacks the vision and drive of real collaboration. Webb and Vulliamy (1996 : 147) found that 'it was certainly the case in our research that almost all the collaborative endeavour was to meet the overwhelming demands of government directives and very little was initiated solely by the perceived needs of the schools and the pupils'.

However, many staff were stimulated to work together by the advent of the National Curriculum and the Standard Assessment Tasks, and while this may have been contrived in the first instance, in most cases the need to work together led to genuine collaboration and a recognition of the value of this. Gipps *et al.* (1995 : 177) studied the introduction of the SATs at Key Stage 1 in a number of schools in different parts of the country and came to the conclusion that the 'persistence of collegiality across time and space indicates that it is indeed *not* contrived collegiality that we were observing but the development of a genuinely collaborative culture'. They also found that schools were using the expertise that Year 2 teachers had developed in assessing children to help other teachers develop skill as assessors and in particular to help teachers of Year 6 prepare for Key Stage 2 testing.

Sammons *et al.* (1995 : 12) also stress the importance of unity of purpose and a consistent approach by teachers: 'Unity of purpose, particularly when it is in combination with a positive attitude towards learning and towards the pupils, is a powerful mechanism for effective schooling.' They note the value of 'the extent to which teachers followed a consistent approach to their work and adhere to common and agreed approaches to matters such as assessment and the enforcement of rules and policies regarding rewards and sanctions'.

A. Hargreaves (1994 : 150) describes genuinely collaborative cultures as follows: 'In collaborative cultures, teachers reveal much of their private selves, teachers become friends as well as colleagues, and if bad days or personal problems are encountered, teachers make allowances and offer practical help to their troubled colleagues.'

He also describes the way that collaborative cultures can lead to real development in the classroom:

> Research evidence . . . suggests that the confidence that comes with collegial sharing and support leads to greater readiness to experiment and take risks, and with it a commitment to continuous improvement among teachers as a recognised part of their professional obligation. In this sense collaboration and collegiality are seen as forming a vital bridge between *school improvement* and teacher development.
>
> (A. Hargreaves 1994 : 186)

He points out that primary teachers in particular are committed to a philosophy of care for the children they teach and that in collaborative cultures this philosophy of care extends to caring for their colleagues. This includes the headteacher who should 'develop and demonstrate . . . a commitment to the ethic of care in their own case as well – in terms of receiving and asking for care as well as giving it' (p.177).

The headteacher is the key factor in creating the culture of collaboration. By creating structures which encourage staff to work together and by involving them in aspects of decision making, the headteacher can develop an expectation that it is normal to work together, share each other's problems and successes and reflect together on the practice of teaching. There may be initial resistance to this if teachers have not been used to being involved but it can gradually come to seem the normal practice.

It may be helpful to ask individuals to research particular aspects of an area which is to be discussed and report on their findings. Another way of encouraging teachers to support each other is to set up a problem-solving group where volunteers meet together to discuss problems they are finding in their teaching. This not only helps teachers to deal with the problems but encourages the view that it is acceptable to admit to problems and that other people may be able to help you solve them.

Problems are often a good way to start people thinking about their teaching, although discussion of problems may tend to concentrate on apparent causes of problems about which the school can do nothing and solutions that cannot be implemented, such as the provision of more money from the local authority or a change in legislation. Gradually discussion can be steered to consider what can be done to solve a problem and the group can be encouraged to decide on action to be tried and evaluated.

Changing culture can also start with the introduction of new materials or schemes of work which can be seen to be helpful in providing something that was not there before and which is supportive of teachers. They might be accompanied by in-service sessions and by discussion about how best to make use of the new resources. As they come into use there needs to be discussion about how well they work and the problems people are finding in using them. The introduction of information technology is a particular example of a resource which can change culture.

Another way of encouraging joint working is to develop an action-research project. This might well stem from discussion of problems and some teachers might like to work together to try out ways of tackling a problem that they are all experiencing. J. Elliott (1991 : 9) suggests that 'issues are clarified in free and open collegial discourse, characterised by mutual respect and tolerance for others' views, in the absence of power constraints on the discussion's outcomes'. Action research may be a way of developing the mutual respect and tolerance. He also suggests that 'Change proposals are treated as provisional hypotheses to be tested within a context of collegial accountability to the whole staff group.'

Stoll and Fink (1996 : 95) stress the importance of risk-taking if a school is to develop: 'Experimentation, trial and error and learning through failure are essential parts of growing.' Action research involves risk-taking and learning by trying new ways of working.

As teachers gradually become more open with each other, arrangements can be made for them to observe each other teaching. This provides opportunities for them to share teaching techniques and for coordinators to support their colleagues with help and advice. Eventually this enables them to evaluate the way a subject area is developing in the school.

Another way in which teachers can learn from each other is by engaging in some team teaching, perhaps for a particular piece of work, such as a project. This is not altogether easy to organise when teachers are in separate classrooms but work could be carried out in the hall for an afternoon with two classes of children. Alternatively, teachers could plan together and then work with their own classes, comparing notes about the outcomes. A project which involves two classes visiting a site together may also offer opportunities for some team teaching. These activities all encourage teachers to reflect on their teaching, which is an important way of encouraging development.

In developing new ways of teaching it is important to remember that there will be times when things are not going well and there is the temptation to revert to past practices. This often happens after about half a term of trying something new. Teachers need to be encouraged to persist with the development since the eventual outcome is often an improvement on what has gone before. The support of the headteacher and senior members of staff in persuading and encouraging a teacher to persist in the face of difficulty is important.

In all these developments thought needs to be given to how the development is to be evaluated and what the success criteria will be. This needs to be thought about at the beginning of the project because very often ways of evaluating can be built into what is planned.

The physical environment

Mortimore *et al.* (1988 : 222) found that the physical environment of primary schools was 'more closely related to the non-cognitive than to the cognitive outcomes, although it was positively related to effects on pupils' progress in writing'. Sammons *et al.* (1995 : 13) note that 'the physical environment can . . . have an effect on both the attitudes and achievement of pupils'. Rutter *et al.* (1979 : 40), looking at secondary schools, found that 'good working conditions, responsiveness to pupil needs and good care and decoration of buildings were associated with better outcomes'.

The physical environment reflects the school culture in many ways. Visitors to the school gain an impression of what the school is like from first entering it. This is particularly important where the visitors are prospective parents. The use of display and the organisation of classrooms demonstrate the values held by the headteacher and staff. The choice of children's work for display shows what teachers value, and teachers have to decide either to select the best work for display or to display examples of every child's work.

The organisation of work materials within the classroom shows the extent to which the work is structured and ordered, and also how well organised the teacher is. This is one way in which the physical environment affects the achievement of children. There is a good deal of evidence that when the work is well structured children are likely to achieve more (e.g. Neville Bennett (1976)).

The headteacher's room also reflects the headteacher's view of the school culture as well as his or her ability in personal organisation. A well-organised room tends to reflect an organised approach to the job. The room also reflects attitudes. The room that has easy chairs suggests a different kind of approach with an emphasis on discussion, although it has to be recognised that in the headteacher's room in some small schools there is no space for anything but a desk and chair.

The impression on those outside the school

Schools are in competition for pupils and the way they appear to the world outside and particularly to parents and prospective parents determines the numbers of pupils in areas where parents have a choice of school. There have been considerable changes in relationships over the years and schools now have to think of parents as customers seeking a service. Headteachers and teachers have to ask themselves about the way the school culture appears to an outsider. Beare *et al.* (1989 : 233–4) suggest a number of questions which schools might ask themselves:

- What impression does the school building make from the street?
- What face does the school show its visitors? What do I see? How inviting, off-putting are the directional signs? [Are there any? Are any needed?] To whom does the visitor first speak? What about that person's manner?
- How easy is it to phone the school? Who answers the phone and what impression does her voice convey?
- What impression is conveyed by the way the staff dress, or talk, or speak to children?
- What are the particular individual characteristics of this school which make it different from other schools?

Some older primary schools do not have a front entrance and visitors can easily find themselves walking into a classroom. What has the school done to help such visitors? The behaviour of the children in the playground and coming into and leaving school also give important messages to those who are making judgments about the school and they should be made aware of this.

Murgatroyd and Morgan (1992 : 50) suggest that:

1 Customers can define (if helped and encouraged to do so) their expectations clearly.
2 Customer expectations and requirements sometimes differ from those assumed by the providers of services.
3 When providers and customers work collaboratively to define requirements and the service that will meet these requirements, performance can be improved.
4 Not all customers think alike about their expectations and requirements but initiatives that satisfy the needs of a significant number of stake-holders can be taken.

The word 'customer' may perhaps be an unfamiliar way of looking at the education service for many teachers and it should be taken to include children as well as parents. The suggestions above should not be taken to mean that a school should override the beliefs and values of its staff in order to satisfy the values and beliefs of parents but that the school should be aware of what the parents think and take this into account. It may also be a matter of selling the values and beliefs of the school to parents, as well as moving to some extent to satisfy parental views.

4

THE SCHOOL DEVELOPMENT PLAN

The school development plan is an important way of implementing the vision for the school. Each of the vision statements may be linked to the targets identified by the development plan which becomes a way of realising the vision and influencing the culture.

MacGilchrist *et al.* (1995) note the importance of recognising the school culture in planning for change. They point out that the frameworks which guide the school, such as policies, communication and decision making, roles and responsibilities are all part of the culture and in making the school development plan these factors should be taken into account. In particular the development plan offers an opportunity for cooperative working. Although the headteacher may be the person who puts the plan into writing, everyone needs to be involved in deciding what should go into it.

Teachers in the study of development planning by MacGilchrist *et al.* thought that the school development plan provided a sense of direction for the school as a whole, a focus for staff discussion and involvement and a planned approach to in-service training. They also thought that training days devoted to discussing the development plan led to a feeling of ownership. Since teachers are involved in carrying out the plan, a sense of ownership is essential.

Purpose of development planning

D. Hargreaves and Hopkins (1991 : 2) state that 'The purpose of development planning is to assist the school to introduce changes successfully, so that the quality of teaching and standards of learning are improved.' They note that the development plan itself:

- Focuses attention on the aims of education;
- Brings together all aspects of a school's planning;
- Turns long-term vision into short-term goals;
- Gives teachers control over the nature and pace of change.

The process of planning:

- Increases teachers' confidence;
- Improves the quality of staff development;
- Strengthens the partnership between teaching staff and governing body;
- Makes it easier to report on the work of the school.

(D. Hargreaves and Hopkins 1991 : 2)

Perhaps it would be safer to say that the development plan may do all these things if the question of ownership is taken seriously and staff are fully involved in the making of the plan.

Cuttance (1997 : 16) notes that

> School development plans are a statement of the key programs and activities that the school wants to change or improve (objectives); how these improvements are to be achieved (strategies); and what their impact will be (outcomes); to improve learning outcomes for students.

Governors also need to be involved in the making of the development plan. It is easy for all the work to be done by the headteacher and staff and for the governors simply to be presented with the final version. They need to be involved at various stages along the way.

School development plans need to cover a period of about three years and to be updated annually. They need to identify priorities and tasks for individuals and groups and these need to be linked to analysis of costs. Costings need to take account of changes such as pay rises, increments and inflation.

Types of plan

The study by MacGilchrist *et al.* (1995) identified four types of development plan in the schools with which they were working:

- *The rhetorical plan* This plan had no ownership by either the headteacher or the staff. It lacked clarity of purpose, leadership and management of the process, and overall had a negative impact.
- *The singular plan* This was owned by the headteacher only and was used as a management tool. It had a limited impact.
- *The cooperative plan* This had partial ownership by the staff who were willing to participate. It was led by the headteacher but the management was shared among some staff. It had a positive impact.
- *The collaborative plan* This involved shared ownership by all teaching staff and some others. There was a shared sense of purpose, shared leadership and management leading to a significant impact on school development, teacher development and pupil learning.

MacGilchrist *et al.* comment that 'It was found that school development plans did make a difference and that they had the potential to make a very significant impact on the school. The nature of that impact, however, was determined by the type of plan' (p.192).

Skelton *et al.* (1991 : 27) make the point that:

> School development planning can be a threat. It can call into question or reveal interpersonal difficulties between colleagues. It can appear to be more work rather than a strategy for working more efficiently. It can appear to be just another way in which headteachers try to get their own way.

The National Commission on Education (1995) found three features were common characteristics of schools where there was successful development:

- a collaborative culture was established for staff and pupils;
- the role of the learner was defined, which included establishing a shared view of good work and standards of behaviour;
- schools celebrated achievement and gave pupils a sense of self-worth.

Making the plan

There are five stages to making the school development plan:

- audit or needs assessment of the existing situation;
- writing the plan;
- implementing the plan;
- evaluating the outcomes of the plan;
- financial planning.

Audit

D. Hargreaves and Hopkins (1991 : 4) suggest that the purpose of an audit is:

- To clarify the state of the school and to identify strengths on which to build and weaknesses to be rectified;
- To provide a basis for selecting priorities for development.

They suggest that selecting the areas for audit is done by the governors on the advice of the head and in consultation with the staff. Breaking down the audit into discrete areas would allow individual teachers or small teams to undertake particular parts of the audit and the headteacher or a senior member of the staff could then bring the whole together. Stoll and Fink (1996 : 64) suggest that the audit might include 'informal observation, interviews, discussion, notes of activities, surveys and results of assessments, tests or examinations'. Full audits will not be necessary every year but should be considered every three or four years and priorities will tend to emerge in the intervening years. Thought should also be given to the maintenance of targets achieved in the previous year's plan.

It may be helpful in undertaking the audit to do a SWOT analysis from time to time, that is, an analysis of strengths, weaknesses, opportunities and threats, with a view to building on the strengths, overcoming the weaknesses, using the opportunities and blunting the threats. Another activity which can be useful is an analysis of the gap between the vision of the school and the actuality. This can lead to a consideration of what might be done to lessen the gap.

Writing the plan

The plan needs the following sections:

- the curriculum;
- teaching methods;
- pastoral care and discipline;
- aspects of the work which need maintenance, e.g. last year's targets;
- the physical environment;
- staff development;
- relationships with parents.

Under each heading the following should be considered:

- objectives/targets;
- success criteria;
- plans for achieving the target, including responsibilities of different members of staff;
- any implications for staff development;
- implementation plan, including times by which different targets might be achieved. Some targets will be short term and others may be part of long-term planning;
- cost in time and money;
- plans for evaluating the outcomes.

Aspinall *et al.* (1997) suggest that:

> if success criteria are to be of maximum benefit, they need to be developed and used in a systematic way which takes account of the pitfalls which can arise. A systematic approach can best be developed by working through a number of key questions in relation to a programme or activity.

Question 1 What is it trying to achieve?
Question 2 What would be appropriate indicators of success?
Question 3 How should data be gathered and processed?
Question 4 With what results can it validly be compared?
Question 5 What other information is necessary to put the results in
context?
Question 6 What conclusions can legitimately be drawn?
Question 7 What action follows?

(Aspinall *et al.* 1997 : 54–9)

The authors also suggest that it is important to keep success criteria simple and clear and to set them after open discussion. They also need to be reviewed after a period. Success criteria can be formative and useful as the work proceeds, or summative, used when the work is completed.

Skelton *et al.* (1991) suggest that headteachers should ask themselves the following questions:

- 'Are colleagues aware of what development planning is?' (p.28)
  It is a way of prioritising the work of the school and establishing what different people will contribute, including governors.
- 'Are colleagues aware of what the development planning process involves?' (p.28)
  It will involve a number of meetings, some joint decision making and possible revision of job descriptions in the light of the priorities agreed.
- 'Are the relationships between colleagues strong enough to withstand the pressures?
  'The process requires an openness and an honesty which some staff groups find difficult to achieve. It requires an atmosphere which is relaxed enough to allow open discussion and an inter-group confidence in which everyone is already aware that the work they do in the school is genuinely valued' (p.29).
- 'Is there a professional atmosphere in the school?' (p.30)
  There needs to be an acceptance of professional discussion of the issues and a readiness to respond to new issues and demands.

Implementing the plan

In making the plan it is important for implementation that there are clear targets which can be seen to be achieved and clear identification of the tasks which lead to the achievement of the targets, including statements about success criteria. This not only makes it easier to put the plan into action but provides evidence for evaluating whether the plan has succeeded. Targets need to be clearly linked to the budget so that realistic resources are available where necessary for the achievement of the plan. It is also important to consider the amount of time any particular task will take and to plan what is reasonable. It is also all too easy to include too much in the development plan for a given year, though as year follows year headteachers and teachers get a sense of how much can reasonably be done.

There also need to be statements about whose responsibility it is to carry out particular tasks. These may need to be linked with job descriptions. If they are sometimes joint responsibilities, this can help develop the idea of working together, although there is the danger that where more than one person is responsible each individual will leave it to someone else to carry out the work.

Targets that are long term need to be broken down into tasks which can be done in the short term, leading to the long-term achievement. Some aspects of the development plan will need coordination and this needs to be a clear responsibility for someone.

Each person who has a task in relation to the development plan needs support. Headteachers need to show interest in how work on the task is going and should be aware of the teachers who have particular need for support in carrying out their tasks. Skelton *et al.* (1991 : 101) make the point that 'when things go wrong, when the process looks like a trough, when it seems unlikely that important targets will be met – then people need support'. They also suggest that planning should aim to fill only 80 per cent of the time available to allow for crises which may occur.

Target setting, seen mainly in terms of test and examination results, is now a legal requirement for all schools and is part of government planning to raise achievement. The targets envisaged require governors, headteachers and teachers to look carefully at their previous results and forecast what might be possible in the future. Teachers in secondary schools are used to forecasting examination results but primary school teachers are less familiar with the process, although many have previously done so privately. Target setting will demand a forecast of five terms ahead of the results children might achieve in the SATs. The information which governors, headteachers and staff may use in setting targets is comparative data about schools with similar intake, having similar numbers of children entitled to free school meals or speaking English as a second language. LEAs, the Qualifications and Curriculum Authority (QCA) and Ofsted will provide information against which schools can measure themselves. An LEA will also set targets for schools in its area. Targets in the development plan will tend to be wider than the targets envisaged under the legislation.

Evaluating the outcomes of the plan

It is essential that arrangements for monitoring and evaluating the outcomes of the plan are built into the planning process. Weindling (1997 : 232) suggests that 'monitoring' is a matter of checking that things are going according to plan while 'evaluation . . . is a deeper study of the impact and outcomes of the programme'. Statements of success criteria help to make it clear what the outcomes should be, but the ways in which these are to be assessed should be carefully considered. MacGilchrist *et al.* (1995 : 7) note that:

> Ofsted reported that recent inspections had revealed that whilst in the primary schools the quality of school development plans had improved, monitoring and evaluating the standards achieved and the quality of work in the classrooms was the most frequently neglected management task.

The authors also found in their research that the weakest plans were worst in monitoring and evaluation.

HMI also found this kind of weakness in following up action plans made as a result of inspection. They found that plans addressed key issues, set out a clear timetable and had made improvements, but only 4 per cent of schools had set specific targets for improvement of achievement and only 8 per cent had developed success criteria to evaluate the effectiveness of the proposed action.

Stoll and Fink (1996 : 72) write of a headteacher in their study who talked 'of the need to spend time in classrooms to observe the effect of the plan on the children'. It is important to remember that a major purpose of the development plan is to improve the learning and teaching in the school and its outcome needs to be evaluated in the light of this. There will, of course, be plans which affect this aim indirectly, such as any plans for improving cooperation with parents, but the overall purpose is the same.

The process of evaluation will in a number of cases be a matter of seeing whether the success criteria have been met. This will sometimes be straightforward and achievement will be defined by specific success criteria. These not only need to be stated in terms which can be assessed but must have timing built into them. For example, the development plan might include the introduction of a stronger element of mental arithmetic into the mathematics programme. The success criterion might be 'To improve the scores of mental arithmetic tests in Years five and six by the end of the summer term next year.' This includes not only the task of improving mental arithmetic but states for which years it should be carried out and by which date. A more difficult case would be improvement in the teaching of art where the success criteria might refer to greater variety of work and improvement in the standard of drawing and painting, but whether this is achieved will be a matter for judgment. A plan to improve the relationships with parents might have a success criterion such as the number of parents attending meetings or the introduction of meetings with individual parents to discuss their children, but deciding whether these are genuinely successful requires a different form of evaluation.

Evaluation for some of the elements of the development plan may therefore require not only classroom observation but discussion with relevant groups, surveys by questionnaire, interviews with representatives and anything else the school can think of. There is also a place for discussing relevant items with children to assess their value from the pupils' point of view. Older children in particular should be aware of some of the targets in the development plan and their role in helping to achieve them.

Evaluation is not simply something to be done at the last stage of implementing the plan. Monitoring needs to be carried out as the plan is put into action and thought needs to be given in planning to information which needs to be collected as the work proceeds. For example, the improvement of mental arithmetic would need the scores from regular tests to be collected so that improvement could be seen.

MacGilchrist *et al.* (1995 : 153) found that:

> A general area of weakness which applied to most of the plans was the lack of structure and the subjectivity of targets and priorities. The absence of evidence in relation to on-going reviews and the implicit limited audience of the document also suggested that the exercise had not been thoroughly thought through.

Stoll and Fink (1996 : 73) make the point that 'School development planning as a process in itself is insufficient to engender meaningful teacher commitment because teachers generally derive meaning from their work in the classroom.' The implication of this is that the way in which headteachers involve other teachers is important and they stress the uniqueness of each school and the fact that 'the planning process depends on each school's political dynamics and motivation'(p.74). Planning which does not take the school climate into account is not likely to be successful.

Skelton *et al.* (1991 : 54) suggest that 'Appraisal must link closely with the development plan. Individual targets must, where appropriate, be part of the corporate plan.'

Governors need to play an important part in the planning process. MacGilchrist *et al.* (1995 : 181) found that 'it was very evident that, whilst the majority of governors felt that they should be monitoring and evaluating the plan, they were having great difficulty in fulfilling this responsibility'. The role of governors in relation to the school development plan is not a clear one and much depends upon the way the head and staff work. Governors should certainly have the opportunity to suggest items for audit, should be informed about the results of the audit and be in a position to suggest items for the plan itself. They should have the opportunity to comment on the plan while it is still in a draft stage and once it is agreed should receive regular reports from the headteacher about the way in which it is working. Committees such as the finance committee and the curriculum committee will have a particular interest in certain elements in the plan and the curriculum committee may want to meet members of staff involved in a particular aspect of the plan to hear about how it is working.

Financial planning

All the planning needs to be linked to costs, both in time and money. Many primary schools delegate some of the budget to curriculum coordinators: there needs to be a pattern for doing this. A headteacher, in consultation with the staff, needs to decide the basis on which delegation is to take place. Is there to be a formula for deciding how much each person will get, perhaps using the amount of time for which each subject is taught as basic information? Alternatively, the school may start from the point of view of how much each person bids for. This leaves the headteacher with the difficult task of deciding between rival claims and seeing that there is an equable distribution of money among the coordinators.

Costing the development plan should also look at the time the tasks allocated to individuals are likely to take. A particular person can easily be overloaded with duties and it is important that the tasks are achievable within the time available.

Contingencies also need to be considered. The sum reserved for contingencies should be as small as possible and experience from year to year will probably help schools to decide how much this sum should be.

Strategic planning

Schools are working in a constantly changing environment. It is unlikely that a three-year plan will remain the same during the period for which it is intended. Weindling (1997 : 219) notes that

> Strategic planning has as its key the notion of strategic thinking which considers the vision and values of the organisation as well as the anticipated external forces and trends which affect the school, to produce what might be called the 'helicopter view'. . . . Strategic planning is a means of establishing and maintaining a sense of direction when the future becomes more and more difficult to predict. . . . In strategic planning, the emphasis is on an evolutionary or rolling planning where the plan itself is changed to adapt to changing circumstances.

Weindling also stresses the importance of taking account of the values of the staff, governors and parents. He suggests interviewing individuals and groups, asking such questions as 'What are your personal beliefs about how this school should be run?' and 'What do you like, or dislike, about this school?' He makes the point that 'Strategic planning which does not take account of values will almost certainly fail' (p.225), while also acknowledging that there will be differences of opinion that need to be resolved by discussion and probably compromise.

5

EFFECTIVE LEADERSHIP

Vision

We have already noted the importance of a headteacher having vision, and this is supported by many researchers (e.g. Beare *et al.* (1989), Bennis and Nanus (1985), Nias *et al.* (1989, 1992), Ribbins *et al.* (1990), Stoll and Fink (1996), Whitaker (1993)). The problem for headteachers is how to reconcile their vision with the developing vision of their staff and governors. The suggestion that there should, at an early stage, be a meeting at which everyone tries to articulate a vision for the school might result in a collective vision which is somewhat different from the headteacher's personal vision. The headteacher's task is to maintain his or her personal vision and use opportunities as they arise to move colleagues towards it, at the same time working towards the collective vision. It might also be that the headteacher's vision is modified by the discussion with colleagues and governors and by the realities of a particular situation. The head's vision is very influential. Nias *et al.* (1992 : 115), in their study of primary school curriculum development, found that 'the head's vision provided the basic values from which the shared educational aims of the school could grow'.

One factor contributing to the headteacher's different vision is the responsibility for thinking about the future. Whitaker (1993 : 16) suggests that 'one of the paradoxes created by rapid change is that managers will need to operate almost simultaneously in the present and in the future, constantly relating current realities to future needs and possibilities'.

Nias *et al.* (1989 : 14) list ways in which leaders 'ensure that the beliefs and values that they embody permeate the entire institution':

- they use personal example and monitoring of quality;
- they select staff who share their values;
- they use language to create shared meanings;
- they help the institution to achieve a sense of corporate identity.

Ribbins *et al.* (1990) suggest that effective leaders inspire by:

- modelling the behaviour desired of followers;
- inspiration, elevating a goal or cause and exhorting followers to pursue it.

They also suggest that power is a tactic in the arsenal of leaders and that motivation may involve persuading followers that the institution's goals are consistent with their own.

Part of the headteacher's vision is the culture which he or she is aiming to develop. Almost everything a headteacher does contributes to this. Nias *et al.* (1992 : 233) found that the effective heads in their study 'sought to foster a climate in which every aspect of the school, except its fundamental educational beliefs, was open to critical enquiry and capable of being improved'.

Primary school headteachers normally expect to do a good deal of teaching themselves, and in the smaller schools they are often in full-time charge of a class. This provides good opportunities to lead by example. Headteachers can also lead the teaching by working alongside other teachers in a team situation.

Alexander (1992 : 149) found that 'The more successful heads were those who remained in close touch with classroom realities and teachers' everyday concerns, who valued and developed individual staff potential and encouraged collective decision making.' Playing a part in the actual teaching provides a good way of 'remain[ing] in close touch with classroom realities'. At the same time headteachers must leave enough time for other aspects of their work, for keeping in touch with what individual teachers are doing and providing the necessary support and encouragement for development work, careful evaluation of what is happening in the school, as well as maintaining a well-organised approach to their administrative work.

Leadership behaviour and skills

Whitaker (1993 : 73) defines 'leadership as behaviour that enables and assists others to achieve planned goals'. It 'is dynamic and future oriented, concerned with improvement, development and excellence'. He points out that leadership can occur at all levels in the school and it is important that others in the school share the leadership functions of the headteacher. Leadership involves inspiring others, supporting and helping them, helping them to analyse and solve problems, encouraging them and creating a situation of trust in which people feel they can safely try out new approaches. It also involves being critical in a supportive way where this is needed and taking a firm line when necessary.

Ribbins *et al.* (1990 : 159) identify characteristics of effective leaders in schools who:

- Possess a vision of what the organisation with which they are connected should be like.
- Know how to inspire and motivate those with whom they work.

- Understand the major operational levers which can be employed to control or change an organisation's course.
- Are intensely sensitive to and continually reflect upon the interaction of external environmental conditions and internal organisational dynamics.
- Understand the fundamental components of strategic thinking that can be used to guide or alter an organisation.
- Comprehend the symbolic significance involved in representing their organisation to the outside world.

Burns (1978) speaks of transactional and transformational leadership. Transactional leadership is a kind of exchange often involving goals set by the leader to be achieved by the led. Transformational leadership involves modifying the way people think and is about changing the culture of the school. Clegg and Billington (1997 : 33) suggest that 'transformational leadership is, in a very real sense, about winning hearts and minds through the power of ideas'.

Nias *et al.* (1992 : 218) found that 'When leadership, whether from the head or from a curriculum coordinator, was vigorous, well-informed and clearly focused, development across the whole school was relatively swift and involved many teachers.'

Whitaker (1993 : 74) defines the differences between management and leadership:

> Management is concerned with orderly structures, maintaining day-to-day functions, ensuring that work gets done, monitoring outcomes and results and efficiency. Leadership is concerned with personal and interpersonal behaviour, focus on the future, change and development, quality and effectiveness.

The findings of a wide range of researches (e.g. Bradley (1988), Leigh (1994), Scheerens (1992) and many others) suggest that the effective school leader:

- is clear thinking, has vision and a sense of direction;
- has ability to see the whole picture;
- is a competent planner and has the ability to get things done;
- has good relationships with people;
- has drive for achievement;
- possesses intelligence, breadth and maturity;
- has ability to inspire and engender excitement about the work;
- has concern with what is happening in classrooms and the centrality of learning and teaching;
- encourages collegiate approaches, teamwork and shared decision making;
- delegates effectively;
- deals effectively with problems;

- sets high expectations for self and teachers;
- encourages active reflection about teaching on the part of staff;
- encourages appropriate staff development;
- accepts professional accountability;
- encourages parents to support the work of the school;
- is well organised and makes effective use of time;
- continues to be a learner.

Leigh (1994 : 25) suggests that the maturity needed by effective school leaders requires that they:

- spend time regularly assessing their own strengths and weaknesses;
- seek help willingly to review their personal performance objectively;
- create a personal development programme either within their organisation or outside;
- acquire a strong commitment to, or acceptance of, the values of the organisation, develop loyalty;
- learn how to handle stress well.

Bradley (1988 : 242) touches on what can go wrong:

If school leaders exhibit inconsistent responses to effort and initiative, teachers soon learn to avoid negative responses by taking no initiatives. Equally if leaders betray a lack of trust that subordinates can fulfil the tasks allocated to them, constantly interfering in the process to ensure that it is being done as they wish, the subordinates soon learn that it is best to leave it all to the leader.

Winkley (1991 : 64) suggests that leaders in school are in a consultancy role: 'Teachers have the right to expect effective consultant support from senior staff – and the head in particular – and there is considerable skill in developing professional and appropriate supports to teachers with different needs.' Earlier he maintained that 'Consultancy calls for self-confidence, a sound knowledge base, highly developed antennae for appreciating the needs of others and considerable personal skills' (p.61).

This suggests that there is a need for training of teachers acting as consultants to their colleagues. In a small school this will include all members of staff.

Motivating other people

An important element in leadership is the ability to motivate staff. Margerison (1978) lists a number of different kinds of influence:

- *Force influence* People in senior positions have the power to insist that people act in certain ways whether they wish to or not. This influence is there for the head of school and those in senior management roles whether they use it or not. It is not a very satisfactory form of influence although it may be necessary to use it from time to time, because someone who is not convinced about what he or she is being asked to do might do it very superficially.
- *Knowledge influence* Influence also arises from the knowledge, skill and expertise of the person influencing. This is a form of influence which could be exercised by competent curriculum coordinators.
- *Reward influence* A headteacher is in a position to reward other people for work well done. This may only be a matter of praise and recognition but it could lead to promotion or provision of resources for further development of the work.
- *Positional influence* Headteachers influence because of the position they hold. Other senior members of staff also have positional influence.
- *Personal friendship influence* People are influenced by those whom they like and respect.

People are also influenced by:

- *Persuasion* This relies on reasoning and is usually the preferred method of influencing others.
- *Exchange* This is a subtle form of bargaining. It happens, for example, if a headteacher offers teachers extra resources in order to encourage them to change in a certain direction.
- *Environment* People can be influenced through their environment. A teacher may be influenced by the teacher in the next-door classroom. Teachers are also influenced by their working conditions and it is worthwhile making these as good as possible.

The human need for satisfaction in relating to other people and for achievement are very important and many people will rate them above salary if they perceive their earnings as being a reasonable reward for work done. Primary teachers generally find satisfaction in their work and this is enhanced by recognition, encouragement and opportunities to take responsibility. Promotion or the prospect of promotion is also highly motivating.

Teachers vary as individuals in what motivates them and this operates differently at various stages of a teacher's career, and differently for men and women. Knowledge of the motivating forces is valuable to a headteacher in helping individuals. Dean (1995b) suggests that teachers may be motivated by:

- children developing and learning;
- enthusiasm for subject matter;

- recognition, praise, interest and encouragement;
- a chance to contribute and to shine;
- a chance to take responsibility;
- a challenge to professional skill;
- the inspiration of others;
- career prospects.

Managing conflict

Headteachers need to be able to manage conflict. This may be between members of staff or between parents and staff, and can be of various kinds. It might be a conflict of ideology and values, about boundaries or simply two people who dislike each other for personal reasons.

Conflicts about boundaries tend to be the simplest to deal with. The boundaries may be physical, as when two teachers clash over the use of shared space, or they may be to do with the boundaries of a particular person's job, as when a coordinator upsets a colleague by telling him or her what to do in a way which the teacher finds unacceptable. Conflicts about physical boundaries may be resolved by getting agreement to rules about the use of the space concerned. Resolving this requires some give and take on both sides but usually people can see the point of coming to some agreement.

Conflicts about job boundaries may be more difficult, particularly if both people feel strongly that they were in the right. This is probably best tackled by a meeting with the people concerned in which the person who objects to the approach describes how this made him or her feel. This should help the other person begin to appreciate the way in which the approach was unsatisfactory and the headteacher may need to go on to discuss with him or her privately better ways of approaching colleagues.

Conflicts about ideology and values are difficult to solve, particularly if the conflict is with the headteacher. Coping with the problem is partly a matter of exploring the values and ideology of the person concerned, looking for areas of agreement and seeking a compromise. It is important not to take a firm stand on one view since this only exacerbates the conflict and does nothing to change the views of either party. It is better to try to agree long-term aims and accept that there may be different ways of reaching them, seeking in the opinions of the other person any movement towards a different point of view.

Where the difference in ideology is between two teachers who are engaged in the same task, such as colleagues teaching parallel groups within a year, it may be possible to solve the problem by suggesting that both work out the tasks over which they conflict in their own ways. It would then be possible to look at the results and discuss which approach has worked more satisfactorily.

Where conflict is between parent and teacher it is important to listen to the point of view of both very carefully, avoiding any appearance of taking sides. The parent must be left with the view that the headteacher will genuinely look into the problem and will come back to him or her when he or she has done so. The outcome may be that one party is in the right or that there is wrong on both sides, and the headteacher's task is to act as advocate for each party to the other. It may be helpful to get the two people together and give each the opportunity to say how he or she felt about the situation so that they each have some understanding of why the other felt aggrieved.

Conflict which arises from personal dislike is not easy to manage. Where possible the people concerned are best kept separate, but here again it may be a matter of negotiating agreement on issues where this is important.

The whole matter of dealing with conflict involves trying to understand the way people feel. It is important to face up to conflict and not just brush it under the carpet. Conflict does not go away unless addressed, and attempts to resolve it may lead to the development of those concerned.

Personal organisation and the use of time

Whitaker (1993 : 118) stresses the need for those in leadership roles to be well organised.

> Those in leadership roles need to recognise the central importance of organisational culture in their own management and leadership behaviour. . . . At the personal level, effective leaders create for themselves appropriate work habits, an efficient work environment and pay attention to their own well being and sense of fulfilment.

It is important to be systematic in many aspects of a leadership role. Meetings must be well prepared with agendas published beforehand which give details of what is to be discussed and a clear statement of the purpose of the meeting. They should also be well controlled so that the discussion does not become rambling. It is helpful to sum up at intervals during the meeting and at the end of a meeting what has been agreed, and the action which is needed and by whom. Meetings must be minuted.

The headteacher's room needs to be an example of a well-organised environment, tidy and attractive. There needs to be a system for dealing with the post and other incoming papers. Filing should be systematic – much time is lost looking for papers which have been mislaid in the filing cabinet. It is a good idea for each paper to be marked for where it is to be filed. This enables papers taken out for a particular purpose to be returned to the correct slot by someone who does not necessarily share the headteacher's view of where it should go. Headteachers should know their way around the files and not rely on a secretary to find things for them. This is particularly important in small primary schools where the secretary is not full time. Thought also needs to be given to the efficient use of the secretary's time.

Administrative work needs to be systematic, with systems for as many items as possible. All activities which recur need to be programmed so that planning takes place in good time and last-minute panic over an activity is avoided. Headteachers need to be unambiguous and make clear to their staffs that the arrangements for such matters as obtaining resources need good systems to eliminate waste of time.

A small study by Dean (1995a) of the use of time by two groups of primary headteachers found all of them concerned with managing their time. The demands of accessibility and paperwork and the pace of change, with new responsibilities being constantly added, made it difficult to control time. All of them placed working with people as their main priority, with school meetings as their second. Evaluation and assessment came comparatively low on the priority list and it was clear from discussion that none of them carried out a formal assessment of what was happening in the school but relied on assessing informally as they moved about the building, talked to teachers and children and looked at work. Their own development also came low on the list. It was apparent from this study that the headteachers in question all worked extremely long hours.

Some time was spent with both groups discussing how time could be better used. The following points need to be considered by headteachers wanting to make a better use of time:

- It is valuable to find out how time is being used. The headteachers in the study kept a detailed diary for three days and were able to see possibilities for making a better use of time. Some of them also recorded how much of their day was spent doing what they had planned and how much was unexpected. This varied considerably from one person to another but confirmed the view that a primary headteacher spends a lot of time on the unexpected.
- It is important to plan time even though the plan will be subject to interruptions. Otherwise priorities might not be met. It is useful to find out how much time can be spent undertaking planned work. This enables the headteacher to make realistic plans.
- An open-door policy often saves time by dealing with matters as they occur but there should be times when the door is closed to allow the headteacher to work without interruption. Staff and children should be aware of the meaning of the closed door.
- The headteacher should consider whether he or she is delegating as much as possible. The head of a small school has few people to whom to delegate but the maximum use should be made of the school secretary and, when available, the finance officer. Some tasks might also be undertaken by volunteer parents.

Whitaker (1993 : 137) suggests that headteachers and other organisational leaders should be using most of their time on the following:

- Identifying needs in individuals and teams;
- Responding to queries, questions, comments;
- Solving problems, difficulties;
- Building relationships;
- Noticing and rewarding achievement throughout the organisation;
- Listening to the experience of individuals;
- Increasing motivation;
- Making small but significant improvements;
- Communicating constantly.

This list does not include work on the professional development of staff, except incidentally. Nor does it include the evaluative role of the headteacher which is an important area that tends to be unsystematic in primary schools. Reynolds and Cuttance (1992 : 55) make the following point about this:

> The factors of educational leadership seem the most important, among them the percentage of time the leaders spend on educational matters and the evaluation of pupil achievement. School management aspects and individual school leadership characteristics are of less importance.

Eraut (1997 : 46) points out that 'Considerable time and energy gets devoted to the assessment of pupils but the information is rarely used for feedback on teaching.'

The school as a learning place for adults

A good leader should be seen to be an active learner, encouraging the other adults in the school as well as the children to become active learners. Learning may be from work in the school – new headteachers learn very quickly what is possible within the school and will learn from observing the teachers and the children. A headteacher may also encourage action research and may learn with the teachers from its outcome. Learning may also come from reading and study and from development opportunities outside the school. These may include formal in-service opportunities but equally taking part in working parties and problem-solving groups with other headteachers and teachers. Teachers also learn from observing colleagues at work and discussing what they have seen.

Other leadership roles

The headteacher should not be the only leader in the school: the deputy has an important role and there is also a place for leadership from coordinators and from any teacher who has something particular to offer. In a small school everyone is likely to be in a leadership role for some area of work. The opportunities and training the headteacher offers to other leaders in the school are crucial to their effective working. They should be acknowledged as leaders and enjoy sufficient delegated authority to be able to lead; other teachers must be encouraged to welcome advice. They may also need training in aspects of leadership, such as leading discussion, chairing meetings, observing other people teaching in a way that does not appear to be threatening, evaluating aspects of the work of the school, and so on. They may need help in encouraging colleagues to try new ways of working.

Coles (1997 : 116) notes that:

> A large part of the task of a curriculum leader is about influencing colleagues. This is an activity fraught with difficulties, but enlisting a colleague's support in a joint venture of some kind avoids accusations of exceeding authority and engenders a commitment to the process.

Mortimore *et al.* (1988 : 225), in their study of London schools, found that the deputy had an important role in the school: 'The involvement of the deputy head and teaching staff in decision making was . . . an important characteristic of effective leadership by the head.' The allocation of non-teaching periods also had a positive outcome. The absence of the deputy or a change of deputy tended to have a negative effect.

Nias *et al.* (1992 : 225–6), in their study of primary schools, found that

> Deputies usually modelled good practice in terms of punctuality and time keeping and helped to generate a sense of 'whole school' by drawing colleagues' attention to school policies and rules. . . . Some of the deputies supported their heads by adding to the amount of praise and positive reinforcement dispensed in the school. . . . The deputies also helped to socialise staff and to maintain the underlying beliefs of the school by applying normative pressure.

The HMI survey of primary schools (DES 1978 : para. 4.5, p.37) noted that

> In a quarter of the schools in the survey teachers with positions of curricular or organisational responsibility were having a noticeable influence on the quality of work in the school as a whole. . . . In the case of English language and mathematics there was evidence of teachers planning programmes of work in consultation with the head, advising other teachers and helping to encourage a consistent approach to the work in these subjects.

Richards (1988 : 18) writes of the role of coordinators:

> In some schools . . . coordinators are now regarded as central to curriculum review and development: formulating and monitoring programmes of work, giving advice, managing resources, keeping in touch with developments in their curricular area, and, less often, running school-based in-service sessions, offering exemplars of classroom practice which colleagues can observe and discuss, and working alongside teachers in the classroom.

Alexander *et al.* (1992 : 47) suggest that headteachers should delegate the responsibility for subject coordination to coordinators:

> They need to spell out the responsibilities and the accountabilities of coordinators thoroughly and provide support to enable them to discharge their executive responsibilities. Coordinators should be given opportunities to lead working groups, produce curriculum guidance, order resources, provide INSET, inform the planning and work of colleagues by working alongside them in class and take part in the monitoring and evaluation of their subjects across the school. Effective headteachers take opportunities publicly to enhance the standing of their coordinators by, for example, supporting or personally implementing developments recommended by coordinators. Regular monitoring and evaluating of classroom practice by headteachers play a major part in assessing the effectiveness of coordinators and contribute to the regular appraisal of their work.

Coles (1997 : 122) notes some of the background requirements of curriculum leaders:

> Curriculum leaders, in order that they are able to provide the impetus for curriculum review and development, must keep up to date in their area of curriculum responsibility, know its conceptual structure, be able to make professional judgements about methodologies, resources and materials, represent the area of responsibility to outsiders, as well as perhaps teach alongside colleagues, lead discussions, and advise probationary teachers.

A major problem for coordinators and for headteachers is the lack of time for this work. Primary schools are normally staffed on the basis of a full-time teaching programme for all teachers and it is difficult for a coordinator to observe or support the work of others if he or she has no time free during working hours to do this. Some headteachers provide an opportunity by taking over classes themselves and freeing a coordinator. Occasionally it may be possible, if finance is not too tight, to employ a supply teacher for half a day to free a teacher to support others. Classes may be put together to watch a television programme with one teacher while the other fulfils his or her role as a coordinator. There may also be opportunities when students are in the school.

Campbell (1991 : 9) sums up the problems experienced by coordinators as follows:

1 *ambiguity in relationships with other class teachers*, whose view of classroom autonomy clashed with the leadership role of the coordinator in whole school development;
2 *conflicting priorities*, mainly arising out of inadequate time and facilities for carrying out the coordination action role as well as more normal classroom teaching duties;
3 *uncertainty in carrying out the role of 'educationalist'*, that is articulating the reasons, justifications and 'theory' of a subject in workshop settings, or in representing the rationale of the subject to colleagues, teachers in other schools, and to governors.

Environmental leadership

Recent years have seen an increasing impact of the environment on schools. Open enrolment and competition for pupils has made it imperative that schools take account of parental views since they are in many areas in competition for children. The headteacher is in a leading position in deciding how the school relates to parents and others in the environment.

Goldring (1997 : 290) points out that the boundaries between the school and its environment 'serve as barriers between personnel and activities under the responsibility and control of the organisation and those outside those domains'. Headteachers manage the boundaries. Goldring (p.291) suggests that:

> The ultimate tension between schools as organisations and their environment, and the challenge to their leaders, is ensuring a balance that affords the school the necessary resources and relationships which require a certain level of environmental dependence, while simultaneously achieving enough independence to adapt and ensure change.

Headteachers therefore use various strategies to manage their environment. They may aim to increase cooperation and joint action between parents and the school, perhaps by reaching agreement with parent groups about some aspect of the work of the school or by discovering parents' views and adapting to them. There is a cost to the school in doing this since it reduces independence but there is also gain in that the parents concerned begin to identify with the school.

Assessing leadership

People in a leadership position need to assess their effectiveness from time to time. Arrangements for appraisal will contribute to this and it is important for headteachers to undertake honest appraisals of their deputies and other senior members of their staffs. But just as teachers in the classroom need to reflect on their practice, so leaders must do the same. If teachers are to be encouraged to be supportively critical of each other, then perhaps they should also be encouraged to be supportively critical of the headteacher and deputy. The deputy especially, if the relationship is a good one, will often feed back to the head the outcomes of particular actions. Headteacher appraisal will contribute to the headteacher's self-knowledge and if there is an openness in relationships in the school, other teachers may be prepared to comment on issues they are happy or unhappy with concerning the way the school is run.

Eraut (1997 : 45) speaks of meta-processes:

> The term meta-process is used to describe the higher level of thinking involved in controlling one's engagement in . . . other processes. . . . Thus it concerns the evaluation of what one is doing and thinking, the continuing redefinition of priorities, and the critical adjustment of the positive frameworks and assumptions. Its central features are self-knowledge and self-management, so it includes the organisation of oneself and one's time, the selection of activities, the management of one's learning and thinking and the general maintenance of a meta-evaluative framework for judging the import and significance of one's actions.

Whitaker (1993 : 147) suggests that headteachers and other leaders may like to consider the following questions:

1 How can I help and encourage my colleagues to express their needs and set personal priorities for themselves?
2 In what specific ways do I demonstrate respect for my colleagues? What would each of them say about the nature and quality of respect I extend?
3 To what extent do I disclose my own personal feelings to others? How do I encourage others to be open and disclosing? How do I honour and respect confidentiality?
4 What formal structures do I create for people to express opinions about their experiences within the organisation? How well do we manage disagreement and misunderstanding?
5 To what extent do I censor my own feelings when I say 'yes' or 'no' and how much is it to do with the need for approval and recognition?

6 How do we handle our mistakes?
7 What do I do when I have made a decision that was wrong and I need to change my mind?
8 In what ways do I seek clarification and search for understanding?
9 How do I ask for what I want?
10 In what ways do I separate my own needs from the needs of the organisation when I deal with others?

6

ORGANISATION

Whitaker (1988a : 38) notes that

> In good organisations, there is strong adherence to a central core of
> values but . . . individuals have freedom to work according to their
> skills and expertise, without undue supervision and excessive con-
> cern for uniformity of approach. . . . A clear framework of support
> and encouragement needs to be created so that the skills and cre-
> ativity of children and teachers is released for the good of all.
> Creating an organisation in which everyone feels a sense of belong-
> ing, a feeling of achievement and of influencing the course of events
> depends upon the synthesising of a clearly understood and central
> core of values.

This is a demanding view of organisation and it requires headteachers both to
draw all staff together in agreeing their values and at the same time providing
a situation in which there is sufficient freedom for people to work creatively.
This is not easy. It is also demanding in the sense that the evaluative role of the
headteacher needs to be carried out unobtrusively.

The advent of the National Curriculum has raised questions about organisation in primary schools. Traditionally most primary schools have been
organised on the basis of teachers taking responsibility for all the learning of
the children in their class. Music was sometimes treated as a specialism but
most other subjects were studied with the class teacher. This had the advantage
that the teacher got to know the children and their parents well and this
helped in matching work to the individual. It also made it possible to relate
different aspects of the curriculum so that they complemented each other and
to undertake work which crossed subject boundaries. In addition teachers had
a good deal of freedom with regard to the use of time.

The problem which the National Curriculum has brought into primary
schools is that not all teachers have the knowledge and skill in all the subjects
covered by the programmes of study, which are very demanding. Headteachers
therefore have to devise ways to use the specialist skills which their staff

possess to the best advantage while retaining as many advantages of the class teacher system as possible. The relaxing of the requirement to fulfil in detail all aspects of the National Curriculum has not changed this problem. It is still important to give children a broad education.

Wragg *et al*. (1989) and Neville Bennett *et al*. (1992) surveyed teachers' views of how competent they felt in the subjects of the National Curriculum in 1988 and again in 1991. The majority (81 per cent in 1988 and 77 per cent in 1991) felt competent in English and over half (68 per cent and 62 per cent) in mathematics. In history 54 per cent felt competent but all the other figures in both surveys were under 50 per cent. Science was 34 per cent and 41 per cent and technology was bottom of the list with 14 per cent in both surveys. With the exception of science the results of the second survey showed teachers less confident than the first. While it is possible that teachers will have learned from experience of teaching the National Curriculum over the period since these surveys it seems likely that most teachers will still have concerns about some aspects of their work. It is asking a good deal to expect them to be competent in so many aspects of work. Headteachers therefore have to consider whether there is a case for some specialist teaching, particularly with the older children.

Alexander *et al*. (1992 : 43) identified four possible ways of organising the school:

- The Generalist who teaches most or all of the curriculum, probably specialising in age-range rather than subject, and does not profess subject knowledge for consultancy.
- The Generalist/Consultant who combines a generalist role in part of the curriculum with cross school coordination, advice and support in one or more subjects.
- The Semi-Specialist who teaches his/her subject, but also has a generalist and/or consultancy role.
- The Specialist who teaches his/her subject full time (as in the case of music in some primary schools).

Coordinators

Schools have dealt with the problem of subject specialism in a variety of ways. Teachers have studied to become competent across the curriculum by attending courses, reading and using the expertise of colleagues. The development of the coordinator role is probably the major way in which schools have attempted to make expertise available. This has created a situation where some teachers have had to endeavour to become more expert in particular areas of the curriculum, and in small schools in particular, where there are not enough teachers to cover the whole curriculum, this has been particularly demanding. A school may not have teachers with the necessary backgrounds to cover the whole curriculum and this has meant that some have had to study hard to become expert.

One way of overcoming this problem for the small school is to link up with other small schools and to endeavour to share specialist expertise. This has its problems if the schools are not fairly close together and sufficiently in accord to work together, but it may make it possible to provide specialist help which would otherwise be unavailable.

Ofsted (1994b : 19) found that:

> Many of the schools were taking steps, not only to strengthen individual teachers' subject expertise but also to make more use of it for the benefit of other classes. A common strategy was to instigate joint planning, largely in year group teams or by Key Stage, and to involve subject coordinators in the long- or medium-term planning of topics and subjects.

Reynolds and Saunders (1987 : 207) concluded that:

> the coordinator's impact on school practice was enhanced by the following:
>
> - frequent informal discussion of planning with colleagues;
> - demonstration of teaching strategies (change by example), often in the coordinator's own classroom;
> - offering curriculum content and materials;
> - 'high profile' head teacher support, especially in juggling time allocation or providing resources, and in expressing public approval; and not least
> - 'grafting' and generally 'putting oneself about' in a non-interfering way.

Webb and Vulliamy (1996) noted the increased accountability of coordinators. Appraisal has led to more of them having job descriptions. School development plans have included INSET for them and specific targets and the criteria for Ofsted inspections have increased 'their awareness of, and anxiety about, the nature and intended outcomes of coordination tasks' (p.83). Webb and Vulliamy also found that 'The majority of coordinators in our sample regarded managing resources as a major part of their role. This involved carrying out a resource audit, updating equipment and materials and storing them in such a way as to ensure their maximum use' (p.84).

However, they found that getting their colleagues to use the materials was more of a problem.

Ofsted (1994b : 21) describes the way coordinators were being used:

In some schools headteachers released subject coordinators to give demonstration lessons or to work alongside colleagues; in others 'floating' teachers released class teachers to work alongside their colleagues. In one school effective use was made of the mathematics' coordinator's expertise: the coordinator prepared and introduced a series of lessons for a whole year group. The class teachers observed the introduction and then led their own classes through the follow up tasks. This process assisted both the pupils and the class teachers to increase their knowledge and understanding of mathematics.

The same Ofsted report also found that few coordinators were involved in evaluating or monitoring the quality of work. Webb and Vulliamy (1996) found one such coordinator in their study. The coordinator in question felt that this gave valuable insights but posed problems such as whether the headteacher should be informed of findings and how to raise the question of unsatisfactory practice with colleagues. There was a need 'to negotiate with colleagues the purpose, process and outcomes of such monitoring and to decide on the focus of classroom observation, how these observations will be recorded and who will have access to them' (p.91).

Whitaker (1993 : 125) suggests four key factors in giving feedback:

1 Be specific and concrete – concentrate only on what has been seen and avoid making inferences and assumptions.
2 Be brief – limit feedback to a few key observations and allow the recipient to respond.
3 Be descriptive – provide only factual accounts of behaviour observed.
4 Be reflective – listen fully to responses, encourage critical reflection and identify ways of improving.

We might add to this list 'Be positive – look for something which can justifiably be praised and if possible use this as a starting point for development.' Too much negative feedback is likely to close down discussion and create a barrier against change.

Alexander *et al*. (1989 : 152) note that in their study where coordinators are concerned there was 'a clear and repeated relationship between curriculum area, staff status and staff gender. Thus for example, mathematics was often led by senior male staff but art almost exclusively by female main professional grade teachers.' They note that this carries a clear message for teachers about promotion and messages to children about where art comes in importance.

Specialist teaching

A choice open to headteachers is to provide some specialist teaching. HMI, in their study of 8–12 middle schools (DES 1985a), found that in about a quarter of the schools children were taught by four or more teachers besides their class teacher, usually in music, French, arts and crafts, home studies, science or mathematics. Webb and Vulliamy (1996) found that schools using specialist teaching at Key Stage 2 for history, geography, science and technology found it valuable in seeing progression within the subject. In some schools children moved to the classroom of the specialist teacher. Where there was more than one class in an age group this made it possible for a specialist teacher to pre-pare the same lesson for each class. They found that generally the children spent the morning with their class teacher and the afternoon with specialist teachers. They noted that 'records were completed very carefully because they had to be comprehensible to other teachers' (p.69). They also noted that 'coor-dinators need courses and in-school support to develop the skills and inter-personal qualities required for leadership, team building and training adults' (p.97). They suggest that training is needed in bringing about cur-riculum change, assessing INSET needs and providing INSET.

They also found that 87 per cent of schools were 'using one or more teach-ers as semi-specialists for certain subjects. This form of staff deployment tended to be associated with rather more effective practice' (p.20).

Specialist teaching leads to better coordination within the subject but less coordination across the curriculum. It is therefore important that the special-ist works closely with the class teacher and that both look for ways in which there can be coherence for the pupil across the curriculum.

Alexander *et al.* (1992 : 21) stressed the importance of subject teaching. They suggest that:

> to resist subjects on the ground that they are inconsistent with chil-dren's views of the world is to confine them within existing modes of thought and deny them access to some of the most powerful tools for making sense of the world which human beings have ever devised.

They go on to state that 'pupils must be able to grasp the principles and pro-cedures of each subject' and 'progress from one level of knowledge, understanding and skill to another within the subject' (p.22).

Organisation of classes

Headteachers also have to decide, in consultation with their colleagues, the ways in which the school will be organised internally. Mortimore *et al.* (1988) and the Primary Survey by HMI (DES 1978) concluded that classes consisting of single-age groups were more effective than mixed-age groups, but for many schools this is not a possibility. The school may be forced by its small size to have two to four age groups in each class. Equally, a school may find it possible to organise into single-age classes but if the age groups differ substantially in size, some children will be in large classes and some in small classes. Here a decision has to be made about the lesser of two evils, whether to have some mixed-age classes which are similar in size or whether to keep the single-age classes. Research suggests that the child's contact with the teacher is an important factor in his or her progress and while the contact may be as part of a large class, the opportunities for individual contact are also factors in progress. This suggests that if the class-size difference is wide, there is something to be said for mixed-age classes in this context. Much depends on the actual size of the classes concerned and the expertise of the teachers involved.

The Primary Survey (DES 1978 : 120) states:

> Classes of these sizes (25–35) performed worse in certain ways if they contained mixed rather than single age groups: the 7 and 11 year olds were more likely to be given work that was too easy; the 9 and 11 year olds scored less well on the NFER tests. This is probably because, for children of these ages and in classes of these sizes, the teacher's perception of the class as a whole masks the considerable difference between the children and especially the differences in their rates of progress.

Mortimore *et al.* (1988) also found that teachers tended not to be aware of younger children within their classes even when these were a single-age group. There was a tendency to regard children who were among the youngest in the class as less able and having more behavioural difficulties rather than progressing at an expected rate for their age. They also tended to receive less feedback on their behaviour than older children and were heard reading less frequently. This suggests that it is very important for teachers to be aware of the ages of children and it is wise for teachers to list the children in class registers in order of age rather than alphabetically so that they are constantly reminded of age differences.

Alexander *et al.* (1992 : 30), reporting on the evaluation of developmental work in primary schools in the Leeds Authority, stressed the value of teachers working together in a collaborative way. They felt this was 'a powerful device for promoting curriculum development'. The possible ways in which this was carried out were as follows:

- a team of teachers worked together for the shared delivery of the whole curriculum; this involved collaborative planning and pooling of individual ideas and strengths;
- support staff were used for particular groups;
- curriculum invigoration – designed to help teachers with curriculum deficiency in particular areas.

The authors commented that teachers teaching together had 'potential to provide a major corrective to the inconsistencies in curriculum expertise and delivery which are such a widespread and unsatisfactory feature of the primary school class teacher system' (p.31). They also noted that 'the partners had no alternative but to confront questions of planning and organisation and hence to explore each other's ideas' (p.84). The demands that this makes on teachers and the benefits which can ensue should not be underestimated.

Whitaker (1993 : 40) writes of the need for a person in a team to be 'supported, heard, noticed, encouraged, trusted, appreciated and valued, informed, helped to clarify ideas, helped to develop skills and abilities, challenged and extended'. The advantages of a team are that these requirements can be provided naturally if the team is working well.

Grouping by ability

Schools also have a choice about whether they organise some work in ability groups. This makes the task rather easier for teachers in matching work to the individual and makes it possible to create smaller groups for children with special needs. Research varies in its conclusions about this. Scheerens (1992 : 41) quotes a wide-ranging American study which found that:

> Studies on streaming or working with ability groups indicate that this type of teaching works more positively with more gifted pupils, and that with less able groups, taking the average results of large numbers of surveys, hardly any effect was found.

What he does not report is whether the studies show an effect on the self-esteem and teacher expectation of those in the lower-ability groups.

Reynolds *et al.* (1994b : 28) quote from a Norwegian study of setting which found that 'students with low socioeconomic status and students from rural areas were the losers'. The HMI survey of combined and middle schools (DES 1985a : para. 7.3, p.65) found that 'no association was identified between setting in English and mathematics and the quality of pupils' work in these subjects'. On the other hand Ofsted (1994b) found that teachers who achieved high standards used ability grouping effectively and Mortimore *et al.* (1988 : 230) found that:

> There was some evidence that where pupils worked on the same task as other pupils of roughly the same ability, or when all the pupils worked on the same curriculum area but on different tasks at their own level, the effect upon progress was positive. In contrast when all the pupils worked on exactly the same tasks, the effect was negative.

Earlier studies of streaming, made at a time when many primary schools were streamed, found that pupils in streamed schools were disadvantaged on three counts:

- A greater proportion of children whose fathers were in unskilled jobs were in the C stream, even where they were of similar ability to children from a professional family who were placed in higher streams.
- Children with autumn birthdays were over-represented in the higher streams.
- There was a tendency for schools to give the A stream the more experienced teachers.

These problems also exist in setting.

The evidence about setting and ability grouping is thus somewhat ambivalent and schools that are setting children need to evaluate the effects carefully. In particular it is easy to make too little demand on the less able groups and there is the danger of creating a situation where they are overdependent and have limited self-esteem. At the same time, setting creates an easier situation for teachers and having a small set for the less able enables the teacher to deal with individuals more easily. The alternative which Mortimore *et al.* (1988) found to be effective is to differentiate tasks according to ability and within the class this would seem to offer more positive effects.

The use of time

Mortimore *et al.* (1988) found that there was a forty-minute difference between the longest and shortest school day. This equates to half a day a week or twenty-five days in the school year. They also found that better results were achieved in junior schools when classes worked at a single subject rather than a variety of subjects.

They found that teachers in Year 3 of their study spent 23 per cent of time communicating with the whole class, 9 per cent working with groups and 67 per cent working with individuals. In Year 4 the comparable figures were 24 per cent, 11 per cent and 63 per cent. The proportion of time when teachers were not interacting with pupils rose from 15 per cent in Year 3 to just over 21 per cent in Year 4. This time was spent on routine matters and housekeeping.

Campbell and Neill (1994) studied the amount of time teachers spent on school work. They found that most teachers spent much longer than they considered reasonable, although there was a wide range of hours worked: from 35.2 hours to 77 hours a week. On average teachers worked for about 3 hours a day at weekends and 9.6 hours on weekdays. Actual teaching took up a relatively small proportion of their time – on average about 35 per cent.

Conscientiousness appeared to be the main factor in the time spent. Teachers with extra responsibilities and teachers with larger classes spent no more time than other teachers. Campbell and Neill (1994 : 170) suggest re-examining the time used in classrooms:

> Their re-examination might include organisational strategies to encourage pupil independence in matters of routine and access to learning resources, the balance of curriculum time, and the quality and value of teacher questioning to elicit answers that might more sensibly have been generated by instruction.

The authors also query whether more might be done by non-teachers and suggest that headteachers need to be vigilant in seeing that teaching time is not interrupted.

Mortimore *et al*. (1988 : 254) found that

> the time spent on communication with the whole class was . . . important. . . . Higher-order communications occurred more frequently when the teacher talked to the whole class. . . . Our results indicate the value of a flexible approach that can blend individual, class and group interaction as appropriate.

Differences in children

Mortimore *et al*. (1988 : 138) found that teachers tended to rate children from non-manual backgrounds as of higher ability than working-class children 'even after account had been taken of their attainment'. They found that 'some teachers have different expectations of children from different social class backgrounds, irrespective of the children's performance on cognitive attainments' (p.165). Teachers also tended to rate boys' ability more highly than that of girls and 'communicated more at an individual level with boys [who] were given more supervision, particularly in the form of extra feedback. Girls, however, received significantly more praise from teachers' (p.167), and there was more negative comment to boys. 'Praise was not commonly observed in classrooms for any group of children' (p.172).

These are all points that should concern teachers and headteachers. Teacher expectation is an important factor in children's achievement, as is each child's level of self-esteem. Praise is important both for developing self-esteem and for controlling the group. Teachers would be well advised to monitor the amount of praise they use.

Mortimore *et al*. (1988) also found that when the children came into the junior school, the average score for reading for girls was nearly fifty-one raw points but for boys the average was only forty-one points. More girls than boys were in the top quarter of the scores. In mathematics there was very little difference between the sexes. 'Girls made slightly more progress than boys over the first three years in the junior school' (p.144). Writing was significantly related to sex. Girls wrote more (on average by twenty-one words) and the work of the two sexes differed in quality of language and ideas. There were no sex differences in oracy or in practical mathematics. 'Girls were less likely to be assessed as having behaviour disturbance than boys' (p.148).

Where race was concerned there were differences in reading according to the home language. Gujerati speakers were better than Punjabi speakers. Both Asian and Caribbean children made poorer progress in reading but there was no evidence of ethnic effects on progress in mathematics or of progress generally.

Records

Mortimore *et al*. (1988) found that forecasts of work and work plans were associated with positive effects, as was the headteacher's involvement in curriculum planning. They also claimed that:

> Pupil progress and development tended to be promoted in those schools where the headteacher requested the staff to keep individual records of children's work and where those records were discussed by the head and the class teachers concerned. In addition the practice of the class teachers passing on folders of children's work to their next teacher was also related to positive effects on progress.
>
> (Mortimore *et al*. 1988 : 223)

This has become more important since the time of the study by Mortimore *et al*. now that teachers are required to provide an assessment of children's attainment at the various Key Stages. Teachers undertake this in various ways, some keeping samples of work, perhaps selected in discussion with the child, some making notes about particular evidence of progress or understanding as it occurs. It is valuable for there to be discussion with individual children about the samples of their work that have been collected, drawing out the areas in which they are doing well and those where they need to concentrate on improving.

Good planning and having clear objectives are also important and need not prevent teachers from using interests which arise from time to time, provided that these do not take over entirely from the planning. There should also be assessment of how effective particular pieces of work have been.

7

TEACHING AND LEARNING

'School effectiveness research suggests that classroom actions account for more of the variation in school effects on pupil outcomes than does school level activity' (Stoll and Fink 1996 : 48). What happens in the classroom is affected by what is happening at school level but the teacher's actions finally determine the achievement of the children.

In recent years the pressure has been for higher achievement in the basic skills and the other aims of primary education, such as social and personal development, are less often discussed, although teachers of primary-age children are very conscious of their responsibility for the whole child. Croll and Hastings (1996 : 8) comment, 'Studies of teachers' aims and values concur in showing that teachers virtually all share commitment to, on the one hand, high standards in the basic skills of literacy and numeracy and, on the other hand, to the personal and social well-being of their pupils.'

Mortimore *et al.* (1988 : 241) comment on the teacher's overall attitude:

> The teacher's attitude towards the class appeared to be particularly important for pupils' non-cognitive outcomes. Enthusiastic teachers provided their pupils with more stimulating activities, and made more use of higher-order communication; their work was better organised and, in turn, pupils were more interested in work; they praised pupils' work more often and also reported being more satisfied with their job.

Teachers could easily be misled by statements made nationally about the need for more whole-class and direct teaching into thinking that what is required is a return to the past. There never was a golden age when everyone achieved higher standards and there is a great deal which has been common practice in primary schools which is good and should continue.

For example, one important element in primary school work which is hardly touched upon by research is first-hand experience. To understand the words of others a child needs to have comparable experience to the speaker. The experience of young children is very short and limited and it is all too easy for teachers to assume experience which the children have not had. Children try all the time to make sense of the experience they have and in consequence have theories or schemata about the world, some of which are at variance with the world as it is. Neville Bennett and Dunne (1992 : 2) suggest that these conceptions 'are likely to be incomplete, hazy or even plain wrong'. The teacher's job is 'to find ways of modifying, extending or elaborating the children's schema'.

One of the ways in which teachers do this is by providing first-hand experiences of all kinds, ranging from things and people brought into the classroom to visits and field study. The younger the children, the more important it is to recognise the need for first-hand experience and to be imaginative about the amount of experience individual children may have had. It is very easy for teachers to assume that children today have had similar experiences to those the teachers enjoyed as children.

Research is beginning to show us that different approaches to teaching are effective for different aspects of the curriculum. Mathematics, in particular, see˹ ˻o benefit from interactive whole-class work and the individual work ˻n has been the common practice of many teachers is less effective. This ˻ ˻ot mean that individual work in mathematics is unnecessary but that it ˻ play a smaller part.

˻earning and achievement are strongly linked to the amount of interaction there is between teacher and child. Where a great deal of work is individual there is only a limited amount of time a teacher can spend with each child, and research suggests that often this interaction is very brief and not at a very high or demanding level (e.g. Galton and Williamson (1992)). More interaction between teacher and children occurs in whole-class activity and this is why the national projects in both literacy and numeracy suggest that there should be a considerable amount of work daily where the teacher works with the whole class. It is now generally accepted that there should be a literacy hour and a mathematics hour in primary classrooms, although it would be a pity if the relaxation of the National Curriculum for primary schools to allow for this led to a less broad curriculum overall. There is evidence (DES 1978) that where the curriculum is broad the work in basic skills is better, presumably because they are practised over a wider field. Most subjects of the curriculum provide good opportunities for applying literacy and numeracy skills.

Mortimore *et al.* (1988 : 228) found that:

> The amount of time spent interacting with the class (rather than with individuals) had a significant positive relationship with progress in a wide range of areas. In contrast, where a high proportion of the teacher's time was spent communicating with individual pupils, a negative impact was recorded.

They stress that this does not necessarily mean more whole-class teaching as such, which was not significantly related to progress. They are speaking of interactive teaching where the teacher and children both take part. They go on to say: 'Some teachers more frequently introduced topics to the whole class, entered into discussion with them and made teaching points to everyone' (p.228). This appeared to be effective in promoting progress.

O'Connor (1998 : 22) reports work by Black and Wiliam who surveyed 600 research studies from a range of countries and found that 'teacher assessment which diagnoses pupils' difficulties and provides constructive feedback leads to significant learning gains'. O'Connor draws on their work to list five ways to raise standards. These are:

- regular classroom testing and the use of results to adjust teaching and learning rather than for competitive grading;
- enhanced feedback between the teacher and the taught which may be oral or in the form of written comments on the work;
- the active involvement of all pupils;
- careful attention to the motivation and self-esteem of pupils, encouraging them to believe that they can learn what is being taught;
- time allowed for self-assessment by pupils, discussion in groups and dialogue between teacher and pupils.

HMI (DES 1985b), in *The Curriculum from 5 to 16*, stressed the need for breadth, balance, relevance, differentiation and progression and continuity in the curriculum. This paper preceded the publication of the National Curriculum and refers to nine areas of activity – aesthetic and creative, human and social, linguistic and literary, mathematical, moral, physical, scientific, spiritual and technological – rather than the ten subjects of the National Curriculum, but the need for breadth, balance and so on is equally relevant today.

HMI refer back to the Primary Survey of 1978 (para. 8.28, p.114) which found that 'The basic skills are more successfully learned when applied to other subjects and children in the classes which covered a full range of the widely taught items did better on the NFER tests at 9 and 11 years of age.' The Primary Survey also stresses the need for breadth within subjects. In language and literacy, for example, children should read a wide variety of books and printed information, including reference material, newspapers and magazines.

'A balanced curriculum should ensure that each area of learning and experience and each element of learning is given appropriate attention in relation to the others and to the curriculum as a whole' (DES 1985b : para. 112, p.44). The current stress on the basic skills should not create a situation in which teachers ignore other aspects of the curriculum. What is needed is more effective teaching of the core subjects. The evidence is that teachers already spend considerable time on them.

The Curriculum from 5 to 16 makes the following comment on relevance:

> Overall, what is taught and learned should be worth learning in that
> it improves pupils' grasp of the subject matter and enhances their
> enjoyment of it and their mastery of the skills required; increases
> their understanding of themselves and the world in which they are
> growing up; raises their confidence and competence in controlling
> events and coping with widening expectations and demands; and
> progressively equips them with the knowledge and skills needed in
> adult working life.
>
> (DES 1985b : para. 116, p.45)

Teaching methods need to take into account the range of ability, knowledge
and skill of children in the class and the experience they bring to their learning. It is therefore necessary to differentiate work from time to time to provide
work which matches the needs of individuals.

Children's development is a continuous process and it is important that
teachers endeavour to build on what has gone before so that there is continuity. The National Curriculum makes this somewhat easier as it is now clear
what is expected at the different Key Stages and the requirement for assessment also puts teachers in a position to pass on hard information about
children when they change class or school.

West (1994 : 82) suggests that schools should have a single generic policy
for curriculum covering work in all subjects. He points out that children
experience a variety of activity and practise a variety of skills across the curriculum:

> As they participate in learning, pupils engage in investigative work,
> problem solving, hypothesising, trialling, testing, exploring, com-
> municating and so on; they acquire new concepts and extend existing
> conceptual frameworks, and they practise new skills and engage in
> their work through a mixed economy of individual, group and whole
> class activities. The differences between subjects lie in the nature of
> the evidence that is cited in the different subjects and the tests for
> truth which are applied in the course of the learning.

Matching work to children

For many years HMI commented on whether the work taking place in classrooms appeared to be well matched to the ability of the children. If we take
account of the experience a child brings to his or her learning this makes the
business of trying to match the needs of individuals more important.

Claxton (1990 : 57) says the following about learning:

Learning is a personal and active process. It is personal because we can understand or retain new things only in terms of the existing knowledge we bring to the learning situation. And learning is active because it is only through purposeful mobilisation of this store of knowledge that new knowledge or skill can come about. We have no other place to stand, in order to comprehend the world, than the platform of our current knowledge.

This makes it very important that teachers try to find out what children know about a given topic before they start on new teaching about it. In preparation the teacher can consider the experiences it is likely that the children have had and the experiences they will need in order to understand the new concepts involved. It is also helpful to consider the language which will be needed and the extent to which the children will have a similar understanding of it to that of the teacher.

Askew *et al*. (1997) emphasise this point in their study of highly effective teachers of mathematics. They found that these teachers were concerned to discover the strategies children were using to work things out, and that talking with them revealed the way they were thinking. The teacher might then intervene to lead them to more efficient strategies.

Neville Bennett *et al*. (1984) studied the tasks given to children in number and language and the extent to which they appeared to match the current understanding and ability of the children. They worked with individual children, assessing whether they could do more or less than was involved in the task given. Where they felt that a child could do more they offered tasks of increasing difficulty until the task appeared to be too difficult. With a child who found the original task too difficult they offered easier tasks until they found one easy enough.

Neville Bennett *et al*. (1984 : 25) defined the tasks given to children under the following headings:

- *Restructuring* The pupil is 'required to discover, invent or construct a new way of looking at problems'.
- *Enrichment* This 'demands the use of familiar knowledge, concepts and skills in unfamiliar contexts'.
- *Practice* A matter of making the learning automatic.
- *Revision* 'Demands attention to materials or skills which have been set aside for some time.'

They found that teachers were giving far more practice tasks than any other and that many tasks intended by the teacher to be incremental were actually practice tasks, particularly where the more able children were concerned. 'There was a tendency for teachers to under-estimate high attainers' knowledge of language and skills, to be very accurate with low attainers and to have mixed diagnostic problems with the middle group' (p.36). Something like 25 per cent of high attainers were misdiagnosed compared with 13 per cent of middle attainers and 9 per cent of low attainers.

The authors also found that when teachers dealt with the problems of individual children they very often taught the work again rather than finding out how the child thought about the problem. The process of diagnosis was often flawed.

Ayles (1996 : 121) noted that 'under-recognition of ability is an important factor in the development of emotional difficulties in children'. She suggests four broad categories of tasks which could help to differentiate work:

- By outcome, where expectation of response to a common task may be set at a range of levels.
- By rate of progress, where pupils move through a programme of work at their own speed.
- By enrichment, providing pupils with additional tasks which broaden or deepen skills and understanding.
- By setting different tasks, requiring higher levels of work within a common theme or topic.

(Ayles 1996 : 127)

Gipps (1994 : 24) writes of the work of Vygotsky who introduced the phrase 'the zone of proximal development', which Gipps defines as the 'gap that exists for children between what they do alone and what they can do with help from someone more knowledgeable or skilled than themselves'. She notes that

Vygotsky's model would suggest that not all tasks should be perfectly matched to the child's current level of development and skill. Quite the reverse in fact, that some tasks need to be able to shift the child into the next zone, *but* what is crucial to this idea is that interaction with another person is required – whether teacher or peer – to help in this moving on process.

(Gipps 1994 : 25)

Teacher expectation

To a great extent teachers get from children what they expect. At a very early stage the teacher comes to conclusions about the ability of individual children and this influences the way the children are treated. Mortimore *et al.* (1988) found that teachers gave more attention to children they had identified as slow learners but this was more often a matter of talking about behaviour than work. Children identified as high attainers were given suggestions about how to improve their work but the low attainers were simply given praise. Askew *et al.* (1997) noted that highly effective teachers of numeracy believed that almost all children could become numerate.

Structuring learning

Effective learning is more likely to take place if the work is well structured by the teacher. It is also important that the children learn to structure their own learning. Kyriacou (1986) suggests that initially we take in sensory information selectively and pass this into short-term memory. It is then processed, structured and passed into long-term memory. The way it is structured and related to other learning determines whether it can be recalled when needed. This means that teachers need to consider how children may structure their learning in relation to what they already know. While this is very personal, teachers can help by the way they relate what is being newly learned to what they believe children already know.

Sammons *et al.* (1995 : 16) describe structured lessons as having clear objectives, careful planning and pacing, and clarity of purpose which needs to be shared with the children. Such lessons also had 'effective questioni_ niques where questions are structured to focus pupils' attention on the key elements of the lesson'.

Galton and Simon (1980) concurred with Mortimore *et al.* (1988 : 16) who found 'positive outcomes to be associated with efficient organisation of classroom work with plenty for the pupils to do, a limited focus to sessions, and a well-defined framework within which a degree of pupils' independence and responsibility for managing their own work could be encouraged'.

The way the teacher builds up the material to be learned in a lesson is important for the children's ability to structure it in their own minds. Building up a structure on the board can be very helpful. Children also need encouragement to develop structures of their own. They learn to use sets in mathematics but this knowledge is rarely used to structure other knowledge. For example, children collecting information from books or a visit and observation about a particular topic can be encouraged to arrange it in sets as a preliminary to writing about it or presenting it in some other form. It may even be worth cutting up notes made and placing them in piles that have similarities. Collections of leaves or plants made during a visit can be placed in sets of those having similar characteristics before they are identified. Children can then go on to arrange the contents of their sets in order according to a definite prearranged plan.

Askew *et al.* (1997 : 1) found that highly effective teachers of mathematics emphasised 'having a rich network of connections between different mathematical ideas'. In their teaching they constantly sought these connections so that children saw relationships and one aspect of the work reinforced another.

Cooperative group work

The process of structuring learning is helped by discussion. This is one reason why cooperative group work is valuable. Neville Bennett and Dunne (1992 : 5) make the following statement about the value of group work:

> Learning is optimised in settings where social interaction, particularly between a learner and more knowledgeable others, is encouraged, and where cooperatively achieved success is a major aim. The medium for this success is talk, which is now widely accepted as a means of promoting pupils' understandings and of evaluating their progress.

Gipps (1994 : 35) makes a similar point:

> What the 'theorists' tell us is that children are capable of more than we tend to give them credit for, provided that they understand what is required by the task; that interaction with others is of crucial importance, as is language; that through language the young child learns, among other things, to think; that through interaction with others, children can explore their own knowledge and understand how the new knowledge they are 'learning' fits in with this prior knowledge. But research also tells us that the adult–child interactions need to be sustained, challenging and extended rather than fragmentary and routine. The picture is thus of classrooms with an emphasis on language and challenge rather than quiet 'busy' work.

Research (e.g. Galton and Simon (1980), Galton et al. (1980), Mortimore et al. (1988)) shows that although children in primary classes commonly sit in groups, very little collaborative work is carried out. This would appear to be an opportunity missed. Children who are encouraged to try to solve their problems within the group can relieve the teacher of many of the minor questions which take up the time that should be spent on more important activities.

Cooper and McIntyre (1996 : 110) state that 'A commonly repeated claim by pupils . . . was that where pupils have difficulty in understanding points presented by teachers, they often benefit from hearing the same point rephrased by a fellow pupil in terms that are more familiar to them.' Galton and Williamson (1992 : 42) found that 'Such groupings do seem to improve pupils' self-esteem and increase pupil motivation, as evidenced by a greater proportion of task-related conversation within such groups when compared to other forms of classroom organisation.'

Neville Bennett and Dunne (1992 : 25) suggest that individuals can each make a contribution to a group project: for example, 'the production of a group story or newspaper or the making of a set of objects in a practical maths activity'. Or the group can work collectively on a project where only one product is required of the group: for example, problem-solving in technology, construction activities or discussion tasks.

A group organisation may well be used to sort out material collected from a visit or from research in books. This helps the structuring skills mentioned earlier. A group may be given a topic and asked to write down the different aspects of it that they could consider.

Askew *et al*. (1997) stress the importance of discussion, whether this be in a small group with or without the teacher or at a class level. They suggest that discussion of different mental strategies for dealing with mathematical problems enlarges children's thinking. They also suggest that discussion by teachers about their mathematical work enlarges *their* thinking.

On the other hand when Tann (1981) analysed ninety-six examples of group work, he found a general lack of questioning and risk-taking, especially by girls. There were also a number of silent group members and some fooling around by low-ability older boys. He concluded that the composition of groups was important.

Mortimore *et al*. (1988 : 230) found that 'Very high levels [of inter-pupil cooperation] were associated with poorer levels in both cognitive and non-cognitive spheres [but] effects upon oracy were distinctly positive.'

These findings suggest that good collaborative group work does not just happen. Children need to learn the skills of working in a group. They need to learn to listen to each other and it may be useful to discuss how you know that someone is actually listening to you. The children must learn to put forward different points of view and discuss them without acrimony. Galton and Williamson (1992 : 121) suggest that 'Children need to be taught how to collaborate by breaking down activities into small-scale exercises designed to improve certain skills, such as listening and handling disagreements.'

Some children need to learn the skills of leading a group, how to ensure that everyone is involved, how to react positively to contributions and draw them together, how to notice when people have something they want to say, the need to reassure and be positive, how to sum up the discussion, and so on.

All these skills can be discussed with children and groups can be asked to consider how they worked at the end of a project, perhaps being asked to complete a questionnaire on their progress.

Both Neville Bennett and Dunne (1992) and Galton and Williamson (1992) found that groups function best when they are of mixed ability. High-ability groups function well, but low-ability groups tend to function badly. When the groups are mixed, those with high ability set a pace and support other members of the group. They also found that groups of mixed gender function better than single-sex groups. Practical activities appear to give rise to the highest levels of conversation but more abstract tasks such as discussing a poem or story give rise to more intermittent conversation but of a higher quality.

One problem for the teacher is how to stand back and let the groups come to their own conclusions. The children expect teachers to take the lead when they come to listen to the group and this gets in the way of the independence of the group. The teacher needs to make it very clear that he or she wants group conclusions and does not intend to interfere with the work of the group. It may be useful upon occasion to tape the work of particular groups and listen to it afterwards in order to judge how effectively children are beginning to work in groups. Teachers need to make it clear that they value collaborative work and it may be possible to use the tapes to demonstrate particularly good pieces of discussion.

Groups for this kind of work need to be small. A group of four is a good size and paired work is also valuable. If the group becomes too large some individuals may either be left out or opt out of the discussion themselves.

Galton and Williamson (1992) suggest beginning group work with small-scale practical activities where there is a specific solution to the problem rather than more open-ended problem-solving activities. The teacher needs to make it very clear what the outcome is expected to be.

An important component of achievement is the time children spend on task. Galton (1995) found that after whole-class teaching the next highest level of on-task behaviour was found in collaborative work.

One of the ways in which the teacher can organise is by teaching one group at a time. This is rather different from the kind of cooperative group work suggested above. Here the teacher may want larger groups, possibly grouped by ability, so that they can be taught together. The National Numeracy Project *Draft Framework for Numeracy* (1997) suggests that there should be no more than four or five of these groups and that they need training in minimising interruption while the teacher is working with another group.

Teaching and learning styles

An early study of teaching styles was made by Neville Bennett (1976). He compared Year 6 teachers who used formal teaching methods with others who employed mixed or informal methods using tests of basic skills and two essays on 'What I did at school yesterday' and 'Invisible for the day'. On these criteria the teachers who used formal or mixed methods came out better on the tests of basic skills than those using informal methods. Bennett states, 'It is clear that overall progress in informal classrooms is significantly inferior to that in mixed and formal classrooms' (p.86). Where the essays were concerned the formal and informal classes did equally well and the mixed classes slightly less well. There was no evidence that the informal classes did worse on spelling and grammar.

However, low-achieving boys but not low-achieving girls did better in informal classrooms and one very successful class was informal but highly structured. Bennett found that 'Pupils in formal classrooms engage in more work-related activity, irrespective of the level of initial achievement, the discrepancy being particularly large at high and low achievement levels' (p.108).

This study has been criticised on the grounds that the sample was comparatively small (thirty-seven classes), the formal teachers were more experienced and the tests tended to favour the more formal approach.

The Oracle study (Galton and Simon 1980 and Galton *et al*. 1980) defined teaching styles and pupil learning styles, and related them. Teaching styles were defined as follows:

- *Individual monitors* Teachers who tended to work mainly with individuals, monitoring their work. These teachers were under pressure and the interaction tended to be brief and frequently interrupted. These teachers represented 22.4 per cent of the sample.
- *Class inquirers* These teachers placed an emphasis on questioning and made more statements of ideas and problems than others. They represented 15.5 per cent of the sample.
- *Group instructors* In these classes there was a fair amount of group interaction, less individual attention, a high level of factual statements and verbal feedback and above average amounts of open questions. They represented 12.1 per cent of the sample.
- *Style changers* These teachers showed a mixture of the other three styles. 'They asked the highest number of questions relating to task supervision, make more statements of critical control and spend more time hearing children read than do teachers using the other styles' (Galton *et al*.1980 : 124). They consisted of three sub-groups – infrequent changers who changed style during the course of the year; rotating changers who rotated pupils from one activity to another; and habitual changers who made regular changes between class and group instruction. Style changers represented 50 per cent of the sample.

Pupil learning styles were defined in the following ways:

- *Attention seekers* They cooperate on either 'task or routine work for 66.6 per cent of the time. They either seek or are the focus of most of the teacher's contacts with individuals' (Galton *et al*.1980 : 143). They frequently leave their places to initiate contact with the teacher. They represent 19.5 per cent of the sample.
- *Intermittent workers* 'They have the lowest level of interaction with the teacher of all groups and the highest level of contact with other pupils.' They worked for about 64.4 per cent of the time and were 'involved in some form of distraction during one fifth of observed time' (p.145). They represented 35.7 per cent of the sample.
- *Solitary workers* These children received little attention from the teacher and made little contact with other pupils. They had a passive role in discussion. They worked for 77.1 per cent of the time and remained seated for most of the time. They represented 32.5 per cent of the sample.

- *Quiet collaborators* They interacted with the teacher when part of a group or class rather than individually. They initiated and responded to fewer contacts from other pupils than other groups and were fairly static. They 'rely heavily on the teacher's support and are prepared to wait for her to come rather than search for solutions to problems themselves' (p.146). They represented 12.3 per cent of the sample.

The pupil styles were then linked with the teaching styles. The authors found that group instructors had more quiet collaborators than infrequent changers who had the highest level of attention seekers. Group instructors had fewer solitary workers. The proportion of intermittent workers for both these styles was average for the whole sample. Rotating changers and habitual changers had higher proportions of intermittent workers and fewer solitary workers. Habitual changers had more quiet collaborators. Rotating changers tended to produce disturbance when groups changed activity and there were consequently more intermittent workers.

Intermittent workers spent on average 20 per cent of their time off-task. Only class inquirers had reduced this group to negligible proportions but 65 per cent of their pupils – the solitary workers – 'rarely contributed to any kind of conversation either with the teacher or with other pupils' (p.152). When working in a group these children were more often listeners rather than active contributors. Quiet collaborators were inclined to act in similar ways. 'Although the class inquirers do succeed in preventing almost all time-wasting activity, many of their pupils would be seen working throughout the day with relatively little individual assistance from their teacher' (p. 154).

The authors conclude that 'it seems from the relationship between each style and the different "types" of pupils' behaviour, that no one approach can claim complete superiority' (p.164).

Askew *et al.* (1997) suggest that teachers of mathematics have three styles. Some are *connectionist* orientated – that is, they see connections between different aspects of mathematics and emphasise these in their work with children. Some are *transmission* orientated – they teach standard strategies for solving different mathematical problems. Others are *discovery* orientated – they use a good deal of practical work and try to lead children to form their own concepts. Of these styles, the connectionist is the most effective.

Ofsted (1994b : 14) list the following factors associated with high standards of achievement:

i In virtually all lessons with high standards teachers had satisfactory or good knowledge of the subject they were teaching.
ii In more than half (58 per cent) of lessons where pupils achieved high standards teachers demonstrated good questioning skills to assess pupils' knowledge and challenge their thinking.
iii In 54 per cent of the better lessons teachers made effective use of

exposition, instruction and direct teaching.

iv In 31 per cent of the better lessons teachers used a good balance of grouping strategies including whole class, small group or individual work as appropriate.

v In 19 per cent of the better lessons teachers used ability grouping effectively.

vi Several other factors were evident though less frequently highlighted than those listed above:

- clear objectives for the lesson;
- good management of lesson time;
- effective use of other adults in the classroom;
- appropriate range of teacher assessment techniques;
- well established classroom routines providing minimal disruption to tasks and teaching;
- good classroom organisation of resources and materials;
- effective planning of pupils' work.

Progression

Teachers need to keep in mind the importance of progression in their work. Children need to progress in knowledge, understanding and skill development in each aspect of the curriculum and there is a need for teachers to consider what constitutes progression in each subject. Webb and Vulliamy (1996 : 76) give a checklist of what might be entailed in planning for progression:

- making links between pupils' existing knowledge and skills and those to be introduced;
- giving pupils opportunities to apply existing knowledge and skills in ever more complex situations;
- setting problems which increasingly require reasoning based on abstract thinking rather than concrete problems;
- moving from working in familiar to unfamiliar contexts;
- moving from an understanding of contemporary situations and events to studying those in the past or speculating about the future;
- moving from the study of local environments to those that are distant;
- proceeding from the study of general characteristics to specific details;
- exploring the relationships between a unique instance and an overarching principle;
- using an ever increasing range of information and information sources;
- enabling pupils to work independently and cooperatively with increasing confidence and competence;

Most of the time the teacher is directing the class and giving out facts, monitoring silent seat work, marking books, hearing children read or doing 'housekeeping'. Only a tiny amount of a pupil's time is spent in direct contact with a teacher and very little of what the teacher does is cognitively stretching.

Whole-class teaching

There has been a good deal said recently about the need for more whole-class teaching. One of the general findings of effective teaching research is that the more time a child spends in contact with the teacher, the better his or her achievement. Mortimore *et al.* (1988 : 228) found that

> The amount of time the teacher spent interacting with the class (rather than with individuals or groups) had a significant positive relationship with progress in a wide range of areas. In contrast, where a very high proportion of the teacher's time was spent communicating with individual pupils, a negative impact was recorded.

Croll and Moses (1988) found that the classes of those teachers who worked with the whole class spent two-thirds of their time in the classroom on curriculum tasks. The classes of teachers who used whole-class work least spent less than 45 per cent of their time directly on-task.

It is important to note that whole-class teaching is not lecturing but a relationship with the class in which children are actively involved. Where the school is small so that classes contain children from more than one year group, or where a class contains a very wide range of ability group, teaching may take the place that class teaching occupies in more homogeneous classes.

Most teachers have always used class teaching for introducing new work, for summing up completed work, for explaining work organisation to everyone. What is now different is that there is a strong recommendation to use more class teaching in mathematics and in some aspects of the teaching of reading and language work, aspects of work where there has been a strong tendency to work on an individual basis. Galton and Simon (1980 : 72), writing of the most successful styles of teaching in their study, state, 'In mathematics work with the whole class appears to pay dividends. Both the successful styles engaged in the greatest number of higher-order cognitive interactions.'

Scheerens (1992 : 42) quotes Doyle (1985) on direct teaching which could be undertaken with a whole class or a group. He defines direct teaching as teaching in which:

1 Teaching goals are clearly formulated.
2 The course material to be followed is carefully split into learning tasks and placed in sequence.

3 The teacher explains clearly what the pupils must learn.

4 The teacher regularly asks questions to gauge what progress pupils are making and whether they have understood.

5 Pupils have ample time to practise what has been taught, with much use being made of 'prompts' and feedback.

6 Skills are taught until mastery of them is automatic.

7 The teacher regularly tests the pupils and calls on the pupils to be accountable for their work.

Galton (1989 : 119) notes that direct instruction is most suitable for teaching explicit procedures, explicit concepts or a body of knowledge: 'It would appear that the more challenging and complex the cognitive skills to be taught, the less effective will be the direct instruction approach.'

Cooper and McIntyre (1996 : 100–1) list the following methods that were seen by pupils and teachers as being effective:

- teacher making explicit the agenda for the lesson;
- teacher recapping on the previous lesson, highlighting continuity between lessons;
- story telling (by the teacher);
- reading aloud (by teacher/by pupils);
- teacher mediation and modification of pupil verbal input to class discussion/board work;
- oral explanation by teacher, often combined with discussion/question answer session or use of blackboard;
- blackboard notes and diagrams as *aide mémoire*;
- use of pictures and other visual stimuli (for exploration/information);
- use of 'models' based on pupil work or generated by the teacher;
- structure for written work generated and presented by the teacher;
- group/pair work (for oral and practical purposes); drama/role play;
- printed text/worksheets;
- use of stimuli which relate to pupil pop culture.

Independence in learning

At the same time as there is a move to greater teacher contact in classrooms there is also a desire to maintain the kind of independence in learning that the best primary schools have achieved. Whole-class teaching can make children over-dependent on the teacher. Collaborative group work is one way in which children can be encouraged to arrive at independent decisions and plan work independently.

Sammons *et al.* (1995 : 21) note that 'there are positive effects when pupils are encouraged to manage their work independently of the teacher over short periods of time, such as a lesson or an afternoon'. This was a finding of Mortimore *et al.* (1988), who also found that asking pupils to manage work over a longer period of time had negative results.

Convey (1992 : 101), studying pupils' responses in the classroom, found that 'In a situation where they were given responsibility for understanding their own learning experience, they internalised the information and became more personally involved in subsequent discussions.'

Ofsted (1994/5 : 30) points out that 'the National Curriculum requires that pupils learn to work independently, but the skills needed for such work have to be taught, content and resources carefully chosen, and the pupils supported by clear indication of the limits as well as the avenues for enquiry'.

If children are to be able to work independently they need a range of appropriate skills. These include.

- *Investigation* The teacher needs to discuss with children the ways in which they can find things out. This may involve asking other people, using books or other materials, or using a computer, particularly if the school has access to the Internet. Investigation may involve making observations, and work in science should gradually help children to become aware of the need to make observations in a structured way. They also need to learn to use the tools of observation, those which extend the senses, such as lenses and microscopes and the tools that help us measure, such as rulers, clocks, weights and so on. They also need to learn some of the tools of analysis, from simple graphs to databases.

- *Sorting, classifying, ordering, generalising* When material or information has been collected, children need to learn how to sort it out, classify it and draw conclusions from any patterns they observe. They may need to work out an order for presenting their findings to other people. Some of the patterns which emerge may lead to hypotheses and the question, 'Does it always happen like this?', which can be investigated further.

- *Evaluation* Very young children tend to depend on adults and to find it difficult to be critical of the things they make and do, but as they grow older children can learn to set their own standards and look critically at their own work. The teacher can help this by discussing criteria by which to judge work and helping children to match work to these criteria.

- *Planning skills* If children are to take charge of their work for a period they need to be able to plan how to use the time. They need gradually to be able to make judgments about how long something will take and they can be encouraged to estimate how long they need for a piece of work and then time it to see how accurate their estimate was.

    They also need the skills of sequencing different parts of a piece of work; this involves the classifying skills mentioned earlier.

- *Presentation* There is a range of skills involved in presenting a piece of work. It may be presented in writing and involve drawings and diagrams to illustrate points more clearly. Presentation may involve graphs of various kinds, or it may be oral, explaining to the class or to a group what has been studied. Drama, music or dance may be involved in appropriate contexts. Children should be encouraged to think of the best way of presenting something and not always expected to record in writing.

Seating

There is some evidence that time on-task increases when children are seated in rows rather than groups. Wheldall *et al.* (1981) found that the greatest effect was on children who normally spent least time on-task. There was less effect on children who normally concentrated well. In a later study Wheldall and Lam (1987) found rates of disruption three times higher and the frequency of teachers' praise lower with group seating. Hastings *et al.* (1996) report a study which found a 37 per cent increase in time on-task in one class of nine- to eleven-year-olds and an increase of 63 per cent in a class of seven- to eight-year-olds.

These studies are all of small samples but if teachers do a great deal of work on an individual basis, there is probably a case for seating the children in rows rather than groups. This is not a good form of seating for class discussion, however, because children cannot always see the person who is speaking. It also needs to be adapted for group work, although groups of four can be formed easily. Some continental schools seat children in a horseshoe, which is a much better arrangement for class discussion and is also better for individual work. Children would need to be trained to rearrange the room for group work, although paired work would be easy.

Topic work

Primary schools have developed topic work to a considerable degree and some extremely good work takes place in some schools. Woods (1994) notes that very good projects create confidence and the development of skills in children, stimulate imagination and creativity within a disciplined framework and help children to learn a variety of communication skills. It would be a pity if the National Curriculum prevented schools from doing some work in this way, although there are obviously projects which are less successful from which children gain little.

Thomas (1993 : 12) makes the following points about topic work and single-subject study:

> If too much is attempted via general topics either important elements get neglected, or tenuous and even absurd links are made to

secure their presence. If a rigid subject division is manufactured, especially if each is taught by a different teacher, then overlap can be wastefully included or, once again, items can be missed because they are assumed to be covered elsewhere. . . . The advantages can be lost of using examples from one field to illuminate or extend concepts in another.

Ofsted (1994b : para. 5, p.26), reporting on topic work, made the following comments:

The trend, particularly at Key Stage 2, towards topics in one subject as the major focus helped to redress some of the long established weaknesses in topic planning. Most of the schools had agreed two, three or four-year cycles for topics. The topics focused mainly on history, geography or science with a different emphasis each term. There was some evidence to show that this brought about more systematic teaching of the 'lead' subject and a general improvement in the quality of topic work.

There was also some criticism of topic work where 'planning referred only to the knowledge teachers expected pupils to gain rather than referring to the skills and understanding to be developed' (para. 5, p. 26).

Webb and Vulliamy (1996 : 59) suggest that it is important for teachers to avoid becoming side-tracked in topic work and they give a checklist of questions:

- Have the staff agreed on the aims, intentions and purposes of topic work?
- What criteria are used to decide when and which subjects or aspects of subjects are taught through topics?
- Does the balance of subject elements in the topic over the year/Key Stage meet the National Curriculum requirements and the school's intentions?
- Are there lessons within a topic which address specific aspects of subjects?
- Are the key characteristics of each subject – concepts, skills, language – taught adequately?
- Is there an opportunity for pupils to contribute their own ideas to the direction or content of the topic?
- How is progression within particular subjects maintained from one topic to another?
- How is pupil progress in the subject elements monitored?
- How are topics evaluated?

Conclusion

Gipps (1994 : 34) notes that

> All the evidence points to the fact that when teachers take as their main focus, individual children, most of their interactions are routine, organisational and low-level; the children, by contrast, get little teacher attention, working mostly on their own. As a result, extended discussion with children about the tasks – including higher-order questions and statements – are severely limited. In order to achieve this sustained interaction more use needs to be made of class and group work

The National Numeracy Project *Draft Framework for Numeracy* (1997 : 2) sets out the findings that are associated with better numeracy standards. These apply equally well to other parts of the curriculum. They are as follows:

- strong leadership by the headteacher and high expectation for what can be achieved;
- a coordinator for mathematics with the expertise and opportunity to influence practice;
- clear targets for raising standards and a plan for achieving them, with regular evaluation of the school's progress towards the targets;
- the provision of detailed and practical schemes of work, allied with cooperative planning amongst staff, to ensure consistency and progression throughout the school;
- clear guidance on teaching time for mathematics and how it should be used;
- practical training and support for teachers within the school;
- effective use of classroom assistants to support class teachers;
- the involvement of parents in positive ways through discussion at school and sometimes in work with pupils at home;
- systematic monitoring by senior staff of teachers' planning;
- the involvement and support of governors.

8

PERSONAL AND SOCIAL
EDUCATION

Personal and social education in primary schools tends to be taken for granted.
Class teachers see it as part of their role to educate the whole child but it tends
to be an area which does not receive as much thought and evaluation as some
other aspects of primary education. Schools may not have an explicit programme of personal and social education, and what is taught may be very
much left to the interests of the particular teacher. This is particularly the case
in the present climate where pressure to raise academic standards is foremost
in people's minds.

Lang (1988) interviewed forty primary headteachers and teachers and found
that they believed:

- that personal and social education was important;
- that it didn't require any particular thought because of the special nature
  of primary schools;
- that it was 'caught' not 'taught'.

Lang's observations suggested that 'this generally held view did not always
match the reality of practice' (p.88). A questionnaire to fifty-three heads and
teachers from primary and middle schools demonstrated a tendency to feel that
personal and social education was satisfactorily catered for. 'Replies to the
question which asked how teachers helped pupils with problems suggested a
much greater reliance on cure than prevention and what might be described as
acts of faith rather than planned strategies' (p.93). He found similar results
when asking how teachers helped children to get on with one another:
'Systematic consideration of school ethos and hidden curriculum did not often
happen' (p.93).

Schools do need to think about this area of their work and identify their
aims for the development of individual children. They also need to consider
how and when teaching and learning in this area can take place. Much of it
may be incidental but some may need specific teaching.

Richardson (1988 : 131) makes the point that

The key areas of pupils' personal and social development should be explicitly structured into the organisation of teaching and learning along with the intentional planning of 'pastoral' elements into the main curriculum of the school.

The organisation of the school and the processes of teaching and learning should be planned to encourage pupil autonomy, self and group reliance, responsibility, decision making and reflection. This means that the staff of the school need to consider in some detail how these kinds of attributes can be promoted at classroom level.

Braddy (1988 : 155) gives the following aims for PSE:

Personal
- to enable each child to feel valued, respected and cared for, helping to develop a positive self-image;
- to increase self-awareness;
- to enhance self-esteem;
- to enable each child to be aware of his/her feelings and to express them;
- to create a secure atmosphere where each child can learn to cope with failure.

Social
- to encourage cooperation, sharing, caring;
- to encourage mutual respect;
- to encourage children to listen to each other;
- to encourage children to be friendly to each other and welcoming to newcomers;
- to help children appreciate and accept differences between each other – sex, race, creed.

Moral
- to provide opportunities for children to make choices in everyday situations;
- to develop strategies with children for problem-solving;
- to develop techniques with children for resolving conflict situations;
- to encourage the children to be aware of their own intentions and the intentions of others;
- to provide opportunities for children to exercise responsibility and trust.

Most schools would also want children to know, accept and practise commonly accepted moral principles which would become evident in the making of choices and in problem solving.

A school needs a policy for personal and social education. This should spell out the aims of this work and suggest ways in which these could be put into practice. It should make clear what should be explicitly taught, what should be explored through discussion, what will be learned through other aspects of the curriculum and what should be learned as part of the way children are treated. It should also give teachers some guidance on the kind of records which should be kept of each child's personal and social development. Like other areas of the curriculum, this needs someone to take overall responsibility for the area and to see that it takes place and is evaluated.

Pring (1988 : 46) makes the following comment about personal and social education:

> Personal and social education requires a particular vision of personal growth, rooted in a concept of person that needs to be examined and justified. It requires a close examination of the experience children receive in all areas of school life and of the ways in which teaching, curriculum content, and relationships shape that experience.

Personal and social education is an integral part of the life of the school. The relationships teachers form with children and the way teachers react to children's work and behaviour shape children's self-images and help to create or destroy self-esteem. The way teachers deal with misdemeanours also helps to shape behaviour. There should be an emphasis on thinking through what has happened and working out what would have been a better way to behave.

Whitaker (1988b : 51) studied classroom activities in 550 primary and secondary schools and as a result of this study suggests that three teacher behaviours are especially significant:

- The teacher's ability to understand the meaning that classroom experience is having for each pupil.
- The respect and positive regard that the teacher has for each pupil as a separate person.
- The ability of the teacher to engage in genuine person-to-person relationship with each pupil.

It was found that pupils in classes with teachers who demonstrated these qualities to a high degree made significantly greater gains in learning. They

- became more adept at using higher cognitive processes such as problem-solving;
- had a higher self-concept;
- exercised greater learning initiatives in the classroom;
- exhibited fewer discipline problems;
- had a lower absence rate.

(Whitaker 1988b : 53–4)

What should personal and social education cover? It is a very large subject but the programme must include:

- *Socialisation* In infant and first schools, in particular, teachers are carrying on the work of parents in helping children to conform to accepted social behaviour and in helping them to control their own behaviour. Teachers need to consider and agree on the kinds of behaviour they want at all levels in the school and how it is to be achieved.
- *The development of the person, the self-image and self-esteem* Self-esteem does much to determine the confidence with which children set about learning and making relationships with others, and schools need to consider how it is developed.
- *Relationships* Teachers need to help children to get on with each other and to learn ways of relating to other people which are effective. Playtime needs consideration, as does bullying and racism. Sex education is part of this.
- *The development of values and attitudes* Schools contribute to the development of children's value systems, to their moral values and so to their moral behaviour.
- *Citizenship* This involves developing good social behaviour and learning something about being a responsible member of a community.
- *Health education* The primary school is the place to start education in good health habits and for trying to influence children against smoking, alcohol abuse and drugs.

Socialisation

This covers a very wide spectrum. Tattum (1988 : 213) defines it as follows:

> Socialisation in school is more than just formal education, for it includes the acquisition of values, beliefs, attitudes, habits and skills essential for survival in the complicated process of living in an advanced society. A function of the school is to socialise children into the ways of society, but before this function can be successfully achieved, teachers must also socialise the children into the ways of the school.

Socialisation requires the school and the teacher of the reception class or Year 3 in a junior school to have a very clear idea of what the school and the teacher expect by way of behaviour from the children. The school needs a behaviour policy which makes clear what is expected of children. The policy should be known by the children as well as the teachers in terms of the expectations of behaviour. Such a policy needs to be discussed among the staff and also discussed as far as possible with parents and with the older children in junior schools, so that it is widely accepted and agreed.

Individual teachers at all stages need to have rules for classroom behaviour, if possible agreed with the children. Wragg (1984 : 67) found that experienced teachers introduced some rules about the following:

- no talking when the teacher is talking to the whole class;
- no disruptive noises;
- rules for entering and leaving the classroom;
- no interference with the work of others;
- work must be completed in a specified way;
- pupils must raise their hands to answer, not shout out;
- pupils must make a positive effort with their work;
- pupils must not challenge the authority of the teacher;
- respect must be shown for property and equipment;
- rules to do with safety;
- pupils must ask if they do not understand.

These rules would apply to classes of older children but could be school rules about classroom behaviour. Younger children would need to be introduced to them gradually as they moved through the school. Reception class teachers need to be clear about the rules into which they are socialising children. They might include things like the number of children who may play in the Wendy house or work in the book corner; what to do when you have finished a piece of work, and so on.

An American system of classroom control, devised by Canter (1979) and known as assertive discipline, involves agreeing with the children no more than five rules for classroom behaviour. If these rules are broken, everyone must be able to see this. There is then an escalating scale of no more than five consequences, which might start with a warning and the child's name being written on the board, and perhaps ending with a visit to the headteacher and a letter to parents. Alongside this there are many rewards for good work and behaviour and much praise, including letters to parents. Rewards should outnumber sanctions.

A school needs rules about behaviour around the school and coming into and leaving school.

The staff also need to think about their role in socialising children for wider society. Behaviour at meal times, saying please and thank you, greeting people, asking permission and introducing people to each other are all simple pieces of behaviour which the school joins parents in promulgating.

The development of the individual

McGuiness (1988 : 323) suggests that 'the greatest gift we can give our pupils at school is not academic success, but a mighty sense of personal dignity and worth, coupled with an ability to operate in a variety of social situations'.

Pring (1988 : 44) makes the following points about being a person:

> It is characteristic of being a person that one acts intentionally, deliberately, and thus can be held responsible for what one does.
>
> What is distinctive about personhood is the consciousness not only of others but of oneself – a sense of one's own unity as a person, one's own value and dignity, one's own capacity to think through a problem, to persevere when things get tough, to exercise a platform of values and beliefs whereby one can exercise some control over one's destiny.

How does a teacher help children to reach these goals? Important learning takes place through the way children are treated. If they are respected as individuals, if teachers show interest in each child as a person, this helps to build personal dignity. It can be salutary to consider the differences in how one treats children compared with the way one would treat adults. There are differences because of children's lack of experience, but are teachers as polite to children as they would be to adults? Of course this is not always possible in the bustle of a busy classroom and children do not behave like adults, but it is a comparison worth thinking about. The teacher is an important role model at the primary school stage and children will imitate what the teacher does.

A very important part of becoming a person is the self-image a child is developing and the degree of self-esteem he or she possesses. Some of this stems from the extent to which the child experiences success in work and play and the teacher has an important part to play in seeing that work is well matched to individuals so that they can succeed. Self-esteem is fostered by praise. Research suggests that teachers do not praise children as much as they criticise them. Mortimore *et al.* (1988 : 272–3) observed that the amount of criticism exceeded the amount of praise, and the latter decreased further as pupils grew older. They comment:

> We encountered a few teachers who thought that the giving of praise too generously may lead to 'inflation' and a consequent devaluation. Whilst there may be a strong element of truth in this idea, and whilst indiscriminate praise is obviously highly confusing to pupils, it remains our view – as a result of many hours' classroom observation – that the system can take much more praise before inflation becomes a real possibility.

Self-esteem is also fostered by the way children treat each other. Children can depress each other's self-esteem or raise it by the way they behave towards other children. They may imitate the teacher's manner of being encouraging and it is also worth talking with them about how it feels when someone praises your work or behaviour, and what impact the contrary reaction has.

Wheldall and Merrett (1984) stress the need to reinforce desired behaviour. One way of doing this is to praise children for good behaviour as it occurs. This is particularly important in the case of children whose behaviour the teacher wishes to change. Teachers tend to praise work more often than behaviour.

Some people have what is known as an internal locus of control; that is, they believe that they can make a difference to what happens to them. Others have an external locus of control and believe that what happens to them is somebody else's fault or a matter of luck or fate. Teachers need to stress to children that they largely determine what happens to them and that effort on their part will bring rewards in terms of success.

Charlton (1988 : 68) says of children with an external locus of control: 'within the classroom setting, such feelings are likely to discourage children from practising the type of achievement striving behaviours (e.g. effort and persistence) which are known to guarantee academic success'. He goes on to say, 'Enhancing pupils' feelings of mastery over what happens to them (i.e. internality) should help motivate them in their academic work' (p.69). He describes a school where the teachers spent a session each week with the class,

> discussing problems that they themselves had encountered when they were at school. Where applicable they emphasised how their own behaviour had created or contributed to the problems. Pupils were then invited to talk to the class about their problems and if the pupil agreed, other children questioned in order to work out whether the pupil's own behaviour may have contributed to the problem.
>
> (Charlton 1988 : 69)

A number of schools use what is called 'circle time', when children sit in a circle on the floor and talk one at a time to discuss problems they are experiencing and possible solutions. A case study in *Excellence in Schools* (DfEE 1997a : 84) gives the following list of the ways circle time is used in classes:

- to build up group rapport and individual self-esteem;
- to identify, as a class, the needs and strengths of all members;
- to offer solutions, care, support and strategies to the individual or group when a problem such as bullying arises;
- to solve disputes through group discussion;
- to accelerate a whole school approach to policy development in matters such as behaviour management and school rules.

Relationships

Children are in the process of learning how to get on with other people. Some children appear to have a natural sensitivity to others which enables them to make relationships quickly and easily. Others have much to learn and teachers need to work at fostering relationships. Quarrels among children are a common part of primary school life and the way teachers deal with a quarrel that is brought to their attention is important. Children need to be led to see the other person's point of view whenever possible and perhaps to apologise when in the wrong.

One of the most important relationships for children is that between teacher and child. As a result of imitation, the way the teacher behaves to individual children may be reflected in the way children behave to each other. Teachers need to guard against their relationships with children being affected adversely by pressures on teacher time or by feelings of stress.

Playtime

A topic which generally receives little consideration is playtime. Tizard *et al.* (1988) found that in the infant schools they studied 28 per cent of the school day was playtime. For some children this is a penance and for others a welcome break. Fights and quarrels often take place during playtime and some children may be bullied or left to themselves when everyone else appears to be part of a game. One school dealt with this by appointing some Year 6 children as playground monitors with responsibility for seeing that children were not left out or bullied. They were given some training and the school felt that the system worked well. Another school gave children who bullied others responsibility for seeing that their former victims had an enjoyable time at playtime.

Sluckin (1981) studied what happened in playgrounds and found that teachers had no clear idea of what children did at playtime. He suggested that the playground was where many of the skills needed for adult life were learned. Blatchford (1989 : 5), who also studied life in playgrounds, suggested that the learning included 'skills like influencing and changing rules, manipulating others, knowing how far to go. They are also learning about gender roles and power relationships appropriate to adult life in the society in which they grow up.' He also notes:

> It was found that playtime could be a distressing experience for some children. Two-thirds of children, girls more often than boys, said they were teased, and many clearly found name-calling upsetting. And two-thirds of children, boys more than girls, said they got into fights, though most said they did not enjoy this, fighting in self-defence, or because provoked and made angry.
>
> (Blatchford 1989 : 6)

Schools which have spent time and effort planning their outside environment, so that there is plenty for children to do when they are outside, find that there are fewer problems. Playground markings, adventure playground building, gardens, places to sit quietly and talk all contribute to making the playground a happier and safer environment.

It may be worth agreeing some rules for playtime with the children, working on the principles of assertive discipline described earlier. It is also a good idea to consider what training in managing playground activities support staff who are supervising during the lunch hour may need.

Bullying

Playtime is a time when bullying may take place. It may also happen inside school, in cloakrooms and lavatories and even in the classroom when the teacher is not looking. Teachers, particularly in primary schools, tend to think, 'It doesn't happen here', but when children are asked about it, perhaps through an anonymous questionnaire, there are a surprising number of cases in most schools. Besag (1989 : 49) describes how the head of a primary school, where parents and children felt there was a serious problem of bullying, replied: 'There is no problem in this school. There may be a problem but it is not a racial problem. The parents and children are over-reacting.'

Research (Besag (1989), M. Elliott (1988)) suggests that children often do not report bullying, partly because they do not have much faith that adults will do anything about it and partly because of the loss of self-esteem which being bullied entails. There is also the fear that reporting it will result in further attacks. Teachers may therefore be unaware of the extent to which bullying takes place. Parents may also be unaware of the problems their child is meeting, while perhaps sensing that all is not well. The school therefore needs to be proactive in seeking out occasions when bullying is taking place. This means being very observant when children are at play, perhaps giving questionnaires to older children which ask questions about whether they are bullied or have bullied other children, providing opportunities for children to talk about their problems, particularly their problems at playtime, and generally working to create a situation where bullying is seen as unacceptable.

Olweus (1993 : 25), who researched bullying in schools in Norway and Sweden, found that 'The greater the number of teachers supervising during break periods, the lower the level of bully/victim problems in the school.' It is also the case that the more the teacher on duty is aware of the possibility of bullying and is on the look out for it, the lower the incidence. Dinner-time supervisors also need to be trained in awareness of signs of bullying and hidden places where bullying might take place, such as lavatories, cloakrooms and corners in the playground which must be visited from time to time.

There remains the question of what to do when bullying is discovered. Punishment for the bully is probably not a good idea. He or she needs counselling about the effect on the victim, perhaps getting the victim to say how he or she felt. A group of children, including the victim and the bully, could be assembled and encouraged to discuss the problem. The victim is unhappy because he/she is being picked on. What can be done about it? The children then come up with solutions and it is agreed that some of them are put into practice. It is valuable to involve parents, both of the bully and the victim, when cases of bullying are uncovered.

The school needs to develop a climate about bullying in which it is regarded as unacceptable behaviour. A school anti-bullying policy, which includes parental participation, is also valuable. Children should be encouraged to report cases of bullying, whether they are victims or observers, and to be assured that when they report it, it will be taken seriously and something done about it.

Blatchford (1989) found that blacks and Asians in particular suffered from name-calling, and Besag (1989) found that seven out of ten bullies had strongly racist attitudes.

Equal opportunities

Most schools now have equal opportunities policies and are conscious of the need to be aware of providing equal opportunities for children of both genders, different ethnic backgrounds, different social classes and different abilities. This is easier said than done. Teachers have their own inbuilt views about gender, race, social background and ability which affects the way they treat children, and they need to explore the way they think about these things so that they can be aware of the traps they may fall into. Presenting other cultures favourably is not enough to deal with the racist attitudes children may hold. Having sympathy with socially deprived children or children with special needs is not enough to ensure that they achieve.

Racial equality

Gaine (1987 : 10–11) makes the point that teachers tend not to believe that significant levels of hostility exist, partly because they have not 'examined their own assumptions and preconceptions about race, immigration, and prejudice, so that the things pupils say may simply not grate on their ears the way they would on another's'. Teachers practising in mainly white areas may be hesitant about dealing with such controversial issues. Teachers in primary schools, especially infant schools, tend to believe that racist attitudes do not exist in young children until they explore the children's thinking. In fact children in the nursery school have often already developed some racist attitudes.

Gaine (1995 : 105–6) suggests the following aims for INSET on multicultural/anti-racist education:

- to raise awareness about multicultural education/racism to help in staffroom discussion;
- to prepare the ground for making our curriculum more

multicultural (or effective in countering racism) where possible;
- to air some issues so that we can see where we stand, as a staff;
- to try to clarify some concerns which have been troubling some members of staff;
- to see if we are meeting the requirements of the National Curriculum;
- to examine the relevance of multicultural perspectives (racism) in an all-white school.

He also suggests that it is important to choose activities which give space for people to talk in a structured and focused way in small groups.

Equality of gender

Boys and girls are different from birth and react differently to situations. Girls tend to acquire language earlier than boys and in school tend to enjoy language-related activities whereas boys tend to prefer mathematical, scientific and physical activity. Girls develop faster than boys in childhood and boys catch up later. More boys than girls have special educational needs, including exceptional ability.

As noted in Chapter 6 (pp.58–9), Mortimore *et al.* (1988) found that girls' reading ability on entering junior school was higher than that of boys with no evidence of the gap closing during the junior school years. Writing showed a similar advantage for girls, while there was little difference between the sexes in mathematics. In spite of all this evidence, 'teachers tended to rate boys' ability slightly higher than that of girls' (p.166).

This makes it difficult to give equal opportunities to boys and girls. Boys are often more demanding than girls and teachers need to be conscious of this and ensure that girls get their fair share of attention. There is a need to observe what happens and consider whether anything needs to be done to ensure a fairer distribution of resources, including teacher attention. Lane (1989), writing of the nursery school, suggests that teachers should observe what children are actually doing, the roles they are playing and what differences of behaviour there are. At a later stage teachers must observe matters such as the extent to which boys and girls use classroom computers, their behaviour when doing scientific experiments and behaviour in physical education.

Equality by social class

Evidence from inspections suggests that some schools and teachers succeed in raising the achievement of working-class and socially deprived children to a much higher level than do others. This is at least in part a matter of teacher and school expectation. It is easy to assume that some children will not achieve as well as others because of their background, and teachers need to be aware of this danger and guard against it. They also need to convince parents that their children can achieve if given good teaching and parental support.

Equality for children with special needs

There is a need to ensure that children with special educational needs, particularly those who would once have been in special schools, achieve as well as they possibly can and at least as well as they would have done with the specialist teaching of the special school. This is a very demanding problem for teachers whose training may not have prepared them for the problems which some of these children pose. A whole-school approach is essential, with the coordinator for special needs supporting class teachers as they seek to implement the Code of Practice (1994). It should be remembered that exceptionally able children also have special needs and require individual attention if they are to fulfil their potential.

Schools must see that children with special needs have equal access wherever possible to different activities, particularly where children with physical problems are concerned.

Resources

It is also important to consider the books children have available and the pictures they give of different cultures, male and female roles, different social classes and, if possible, people with special needs. Taverner (1990 : 30) makes the following statement:

> Reading materials which show ethnic minority characters in positive and respected ways are able to counter stereotyped images. This is further supported by those books which take the variety of cultures for granted and accept them as a natural part of our society. Those characters need to be seen as taking a full part in the everyday lives of children and adults and sharing in common and commonplace reactions. At the same time, however, there is a need for books to inform their readers, in a balanced and accurate way, of the special experiences of children of different cultures.

Similar points might be made about the image books give of the roles in society of men and women. They need to show that men can undertake roles such as caring for children and that women can aspire to most of the roles that were formerly the province of men. At the same time it must be recognised that both sexes have particular contributions to make because of their biological make-ups.

Sex education

Sex education is an area of the curriculum which teachers often find difficult and from which parents may choose to withdraw their children. In practice very few do take up this option but the whole area is very sensitive, with the school needing to work closely with parents, explaining what the teachers are doing and requesting parental support.

Children are now aware of sex in a way they were not in previous generations. Went (1988 : 279–80) suggests a wide range of aims for sex education, including the following:

- to generate an atmosphere where questions about reproduction can be asked and answered without embarrassment on either side;
- to provide acceptable vocabulary for all parts of the body;
- to counteract myths and folklore;
- to elucidate the nature of human reproduction in gradually increasing detail;
- to stress the value of family life (taken in its widest definition) and the need for proper care for all young things;
- to help children understand that they have rights, and should have control over who touches their bodies and to increase communication about these;
- to aid communication about forthcoming pubertal changes.

Stressing the value of family life involves the whole area of relationships and this can be discussed in a wider way. Questions such as 'What makes people like another person?', 'How do you make friends with someone?', ' What is the best way to deal with someone who is being nasty to you?', 'How should you behave when you feel annoyed with someone?' are highly relevant to children at the primary school stage and yet will still be relevant later when they come to have sexual relationships.

The development of values and attitudes

School contributes to the value system each child is forming during childhood and adolescence. Parents are the primary source of values for children but school makes an important contribution. If the school is to make a positive contribution, it is important that teachers are in broad agreement about the values they are promulgating. Values need discussion and formulation as much as vision. This may not be easy in that there can be very different views from different people, but there will probably be enough agreement to form a basis for a statement. Once this is done, the staff can begin to think about how they can influence the children to hold certain values.

Pring (1988 : 43) stresses the need for reflection on values and makes the following comment:

> One characteristic of being a person is the capacity to think, to reflect, to make sense of one's experience, to engage critically with the received values, beliefs and assumptions that one is confronted with – the development, in other words, of the *powers* of the mind.

He also says that 'the capacity to engage in critical reflection upon generally accepted beliefs' requires nurturing over a long period and 'will affect the way authority is exercised within the school' (p.42).

Important aspects of this work are children's moral values. Moral education cannot be simply a matter of teaching what is right and wrong. Sometimes people talk as if morality were simply a matter of obeying a set of rules which are universally accepted. It is much more complicated than this. It is wrong to kill another person, except in wartime, when it may appear virtuous. It is wrong to lie, but many of us would accept that there are situations when to tell the truth would be an offence against love. It is wrong to steal, but many quite moral people accept that a large organisation can do without a bit of stationery or a biro.

It is also the case that in real life moral questions are not always posed in a straightforward way. Often we meet a situation which is complex and where it is difficult to separate right from wrong. Nevertheless, we recognise that there is a kind of behaviour to which we give the name moral. Wilson *et al*. (1967) give the following list of criteria for assessing whether an opinion is moral:

- It must be freely held. Moral behaviour must be intentional.
- It must be rational. The individual must be acting as he or she is because he or she has thought about the situation.
- It must be impartial between persons. One cannot have a moral code which is variable between people, although in practice this often happens.
- It must be prescriptive. When a person behaves in a moral way, he or she does so as a result of holding a moral principle which would result in similar action in a similar situation.
- It must be overriding and take precedence over the individual's other opinions.

The same authors give a list of moral components – contributory factors to the ability to act in a moral way:

- Ability to identify with others.
- Insight into one's own feelings and those of others and capacity to describe them correctly. Self-knowledge.
- Mastery of the relevant facts in a situation.

- The rational formulation of this knowledge into general rules for behaviour.
- The rational formulation of rules for one's own life and interests.
- The capacity to put these rules into action.

Young children learn gradually that certain behaviours are pleasing to the adults in their lives and others displeasing, and they tend to make and act upon generalisations about this at an early age. In the course of this learning they take as their own many of the rules which the adults in their world lay down. This is the basis of conscience. Moral behaviour begins to develop when they progress out of the egocentric stage, where everything revolves around self, and move on to a stage where they are able to see from another person's point of view. Morality then becomes a matter of behaving in certain ways because of one's obligations to others.

The moral climate of the school is of considerable importance. The adults who set the pattern should be seen to behave in certain ways. They need to be seen to be cooperative and ready to discuss problems with each other and with the children. The children should see in the relationships of their teachers examples of kindness, thoughtfulness and consideration, as well as readiness to accept differences of view. Children should be encouraged to think through moral situations, some of which will arise in day-to-day living. Others may be introduced from stories, perhaps from newspapers or from children's literature.

The moral components given earlier provide a basis for moral education. Teachers can help children to see from the point of view of others in many ways. They can help children to think through moral situations and start making rules for themselves about right behaviour.

Citizenship

What is involved in being a good citizen? Many of the points made in other sections of this chapter are relevant here. The good citizen is moral, has good relationships with others and is considerate. He or she also cares about the environment and is in some sense a citizen of the world, with sympathy for the problems of Third World countries and the poor and disadvantaged in our own society. These concerns arise from knowledge and from attitudes developed in the process of acquiring that knowledge. It is all part of developing a value system. Schools help to develop these values by what they teach and by the way good relationships and thoughtful attitudes are encouraged.

Good citizens know something of the way in which the country is governed, and local and national elections offer an opportunity for teaching about the way we are represented and people are chosen to be local councillors and Members of Parliament, especially if the school is being used as a polling station. Schools need to be concerned with preparing children for life in a democracy. Day-to-day news may offer opportunities for talking to children about what is going on and its relevance for them.

The National Curriculum requires schools to teach about the environment and how people affect it. Today's children need to be aware of the results of global warming and the damage we are doing to our environment. They should be given opportunities to consider environmental problems, such as deciding where to site new roads or housing developments and new communities as the population increases. Much work in the geography curriculum has implications for citizenship.

Children must also be concerned about their local environment and encouraged to look after their school environment, avoiding damage and keeping it free from graffiti and litter. This will help to create attitudes towards graffiti and litter in the surrounding environment. They should also be taught of the ways in which the environment is changing all the time.

The National Curriculum in geography requires the study of places and themes about different societies in various geographical locations. This should provide an opportunity for teaching about European countries and the Third World. The Internet provides opportunities for making links with other countries and further contacts can be made through ordinary correspondence.

Another aspect of citizenship is that children should learn to be answerable for their own behaviour to become responsible people. Schools often give practice in being responsible to those children who have shown that they can behave conscientiously, while other children who are less responsible in behaviour get less practice. Schools need to think about how they train children to become responsible people, so that all children develop the necessary skills. Richardson (1988 : 132) makes the following comment:

> The organisation of the school and the process of teaching and learning should be planned to encourage pupils' autonomy, self and group reliance, responsibility, decision making and reflection. This means that the staff of the school need to consider in some detail how these kinds of attributes can be promoted at classroom level.

A further area which should be considered is that of business and its role in the country's economic situation. This might be pursued in relation to a contact with a local industry. Opportunities to visit a manufacturing concern give children insights into how factories work and follow-up discussion can involve considering how manufacturing businesses acquire raw materials and control output and the financial implications of this.

Health education

Health education should be part of the curriculum from the beginning. Wetton and Moon (1988 : 95) put it this way:

> For health education to be effective, valued and valuable, it must be

planned and practised as a broad-based programme which starts with the youngest children in the school, takes account of what they bring to their own learning and builds up – and on – their experiences, their explanations, their personal language.

The authors go on to stress that health education must be planned but can include spontaneous work arising from situations. It needs to be flexible, simple and holistic, exploring the way our bodies work, change and grow. Wetton and Moon also suggest that the work should reach out and 'draw on the expertise and knowledge of the children's families' (p.99).

Health education in primary schools should cover the body's needs for keeping healthy – adequate sleep, healthy eating and exercise – encouraging children to form good habits. It should also cover the way children's bodies will develop in adolescence and here it links with sex education.

An important part of the programme is to lay the foundations of views about smoking, drugs and alcohol. Children must learn when they are young to say no to smoking and drugs and to accept that alcohol should be taken in moderation. The evidence is that many children encounter the temptation to smoke and take drugs while they are still in the primary school, so teaching about avoidance must start early.

Conclusion

The difficulty about personal and social education at the primary stage is not what to teach but when. The programme for primary schools is overcrowded and it is difficult to fit in specific teaching about personal and social skills.

One approach is to consider what is specified in the National Curriculum which leads into some of the teaching required for personal and social development. There is much which can be adapted to provide a suitable programme. The science curriculum at Key Stage 1, for example, involves teaching about human beings as organisms and study of what is required for healthy living. This is developed further at Key Stage 2, which specifically includes teaching about the teeth and the importance of dental care. The geography curriculum includes much work on the environment. Studying books in English may lead to discussion about the way the characters in stories manage their lives and how to deal with social problems.

Another way of approaching personal and social education is to consider what is learned incidentally from the way children are treated and the way misdemeanours are dealt with. Braddy (1988), for example, suggests that the teacher might encourage positive peer support, attitudes and activities to make children responsible to and for themselves. She also suggests encouraging reflection. Much can be learned through discussion, both as a class and in small groups.

9

MANAGING CHANGE

However well a school is doing, it is likely that it will need to experience change in the years ahead. New materials will be produced, teachers will have ideas about better ways of doing things, research will identify more effective methods of working and there will inevitably be further changes required by the government. A school which is not changing in some way is not developing. All schools need to manage change so that teachers do not feel deskilled.

Clegg and Billington (1997 : 23) stress the need for managing constant change:

> It is the responsibility of the headteacher to manage an environment fraught with potential problems in a way which promotes constant change as the norm. To achieve this means working with and through people and also means to a larger extent relinquishing the notion that you can control what others are doing. It means supporting, encouraging and arguing with people as they seek to improve and develop what they are doing.

Fullan (1992 : 27) suggests that 'successful school improvement . . . depends on an understanding of the problem of change at the level of practice and the development of corresponding strategies for bringing about beneficial reforms'.

Change is difficult because it may require a rethinking of the values and attitudes that teachers hold about the work they do. Rudduck (1991 : 31) points out that 'if change is seen as a denial of a person's professional past, then his or her investment in a change programme will be at most slender. . . . Change can threaten the basis of one's identity.' The way some politicians and the media have dealt with the need for change in schools is undoubtedly threatening to teachers and is an example of how not to persuade people of the need for change. Fortunately most primary teachers are resilient and it is much to their credit that they have dealt with the many changes in recent years in a highly professional way.

Rudduck (1991) also suggests that teachers need to be clear about their values and discuss these in the context of change. Some of the problems schools

have faced arise from the difference in values between politicians and tea
She suggests that schools should be prepared to tackle issues of values co
oratively, for unless there is exploration of values and purposes in working
groups, coherent whole-school change is unlikely to be achieved.

Hopkins (1993 : 14) makes the point that

> In many of our most successful schools, there is a recognition that the
> social aspects of change are at least as important as the more techni-
> cal emphasis on prioritisation and strategic planning. It is through
> such an approach to school development that recognises the social
> complexity of change that some schools are managing to achieve qual-
> ity in times of change.

What we can conclude from research and from the current climate is that
schools must accept that there is always room for improvement. Demands for
change will continue and even escalate, and schools must learn to deal with
such demands by clarifying their thinking about particular changes.
Developments should be accommodated within existing values and schools
must always be amenable to change.

Fullan (1992 : 25) notes that research about change suggests four main
insights. It requires:

- active initiation and participation;
- pressure and support;
- changes in behaviour and beliefs;
- the overriding problem of ownership.

He points out that 'most people do not discover new understandings until they
have delved into something. In many cases changes in behaviour precede
rather than follow changes in belief.' He notes that ownership is not acquired
easily and 'Ownership in the sense of clarity, skill and commitment is a pro-
gressive process' (p.25).

Change very often involves changing the culture of the school in some
respect and it may challenge deeply held beliefs of teachers who will need considerable help and support to cope with the new demands.

Lewis (1985 : 149) notes that:

> Change can also be produced where knowledge is seen as not so much
> new information about the external world but rather new information
> about the internal world – expanded self-awareness, self-understand-
> ing and self-control. Many of our actions both personally and
> professionally are based on our individual commitment to and inter-
> nalising of norms of which we are unconscious.

School improvement and the changes involved are long-term processes which need to be carefully planned and implemented over a period of years. The search for improvement never comes to an end, so that schools need to recognise that change of some kind will be continual. Change is a process rather than an event.

Fullan and Stiegelbauer (1991 : 127–8) suggest that teachers use four main criteria in assessing change:

1 Does that change potentially address a need? Will students be interested? Will they learn? Is there evidence that the change works? i.e that it produces the claimed results?
2 How clear is the change in terms of what the teacher will have to do?
3 How will it affect the teacher personally in terms of time, energy, new skills, sense of excitement and competence and interference with existing priorities?
4 How rewarding will the experience be in terms of interaction with peers or others?

The role of the headteacher

The headteacher has a key role in leading change. He or she may be the change agent or may be implementing changes suggested by someone else or required by law. On many occasions it will be the task of the head to start people thinking about the possibility of change. The headteacher can also help to develop a climate in the school in which there is an interest in development, and some change is a normal part of the way the school operates. He or she must seek out the best starting points, spend time talking with teachers about the best way of proceeding, coordinate the plans for change, see that there is appropriate staff development activity and that the changes, when implemented, are monitored, followed up and maintained.

Headteachers need to be conscious of the fact that it is tempting when first appointed to want to make changes too quickly. It is also easy when the initial changes are made successfully and the school is running on an even keel to feel that further changes are not needed. Even if external demands for change allow this, the developing school should be continually looking for ways to develop further.

Fullan and Stiegelbauer (1991 : 76), writing of the situation in Canada, comment that 'The principal's actions serve to legitimate whether a change is to be taken seriously and to support teachers both psychologically and with resources.' They go on to say, 'The principal is the person most likely to be in a position to shape the organisational conditions necessary for success, such as the development of shared goals, collaborative work structure and climate and procedures for monitoring results.'

The headteacher makes decisions about how other people become part of the change process. There are three ways of doing this and it is wise to be clear which of the three is being employed because people like to know where they stand.

- *Other people can be involved* Involving people in a decision means actually letting them make the decision and standing by their conclusions. It is a good idea to state clearly in the first instance the parameters within which the decision is being made and the conclusions which would be unacceptable.
- *Other people can be consulted* In this context a decision is being discussed with people but will eventually be taken by the head, the governors or the whole staff group.
- *Other people can be informed* Not everyone can be involved or consulted about any particular change and there will always be people who need to know that the change is being made but are not part of the decision-making process. Parents may very well be in this group, as will the children.

Planning and implementing change

Identifying changes

The first task is to identify the changes needed. These may be dictated from outside the school, or identified by an inspection, but many changes will be those the headteacher or staff see are needed. It is a good idea to try to put into words exactly what needs to be changed. It helps to write this in two columns, the first giving the present situation and the second the situation which is desirable. For example:

Mathematics teaching is mainly done on an individual basis.	There should be more interactive whole-class or group work.

Setting it out in this way helps to identify exactly what is needed to change practice and gives criteria for evaluation when the change has been implemented.

Assessing the situation

The next task is to assess the situation, looking at what is likely to pose problems and at the best way to tackle them. It can be helpful to identify the preconditions for change. There are a number of preconditions common to most changes and others which may be relevant to the particular school. The common ones are listed in Figure 9.1.

The first column should be completed putting down a lettered grade to represent the importance of this aspect for the particular innovation being considered. The five columns on the other side are to assess the situation as it is on the ground so far as any particular project is concerned. If there are many items where the grade is high but the state of things is low it may be better to postpone the innovation until the situation has improved and to work at improving it in the meantime.

Grade	Preconditions	++	+	av	–	– –
	Motivation of those involved					
	Experience of those involved					
	Ability/skill of those involved					
	Knowledge of those involved					
	Attitudes of teachers					
	Attitudes of children					
	Attitudes of governors					
	Attitudes of parents and community					
	Relationships: teacher/teacher					
	Relationships: teacher/headteacher					
	Relationships: teachers/children					
	Relationships: school/parents					
	Resources: space					
	Resources: time					
	Resources: materials/equipment					
	Other preconditions					

Figure 9.1 Preconditions for change

We have already noted that change can be traumatic and this means that it is important to implement planned change very carefully, preparing the ground by talking to individuals and perhaps starting with one or two people who are keen to try the changes suggested. Sometimes an occasion will arise when a teacher comes up with a problem to which the change the headteacher has in mind offers a solution. Hopkins (1993 : 134) suggests the following conditions for effective change:

- a commitment to staff development;
- practical efforts to involve staff, students and the community in school policies and decisions;
- effective leadership, but not just of the head – the leadership function is spread throughout the school;
- effective coordination strategies;
- proper attention to the potential benefits of enquiry and reflection;
- a commitment to collaborative planning activity.

The best place to start making changes is where people see a need for change or where they see a problem. It is not always possible to work in this way because sometimes changes are required from above and then it is a matter of supporting and encouraging people as they find their way round different demands. But, where possible, talking through people's problems leads to changes which make sense to them, because they will feel ownership of what they have helped to suggest. It may be helpful to spend an in-service day thinking through the problems people have identified and their implications, perhaps involving a consultant or an adviser to help with setting out possible ways of working and talking about any relevant research.

Strategies for change

Once people come to see change not just as something forced upon them from outside but as a normal part of the working of the school, it becomes possible to work together and plan ahead. The following may be useful strategies:

1 Ask people what they would like to change and start with these ideas. People will certainly come up with ideas about which nothing can be done but there will also be some useful starting points.
2 Create situations which bring people up against a need for change. For example, a teacher or group of teachers might be asked to study a particular problem in the school or teach a group which poses specific problems.
3 Arrange visits to another school where seeing some proposed changes in action may generate enthusiasm.
4 Make change attractive by putting resources into it.
5 Establish working groups with a task to do. Make sure that the group

contains some people who are likely to be open-minded about change so that they may influence others in the group.

6   Invite people who have something to offer to pioneer changes. It is important that such changes are successful, because their success will influence the readiness of others to make changes.

7   Create situations in which people will want to be seen to do well. For example, a small group or a postholder could be invited to research something and report to a staff meeting.

8   See if it is possible to organise so that someone is released from teaching for a period to work at a particular change on behalf of others. for example, the head might offer to take a teacher's class every morning for a week so that the teacher concerned could get something done for the school.

9   Use brainstorming in a staff group to generate ideas for dealing with an accepted problem.

10 Break up the topic under discussion into as many sections as there are people in the group. Write each one of these at the top of an overhead projector transparency. Pass these round the group asking everyone to write down an idea for dealing with the topic at the head of the transparency. When everyone has exhausted ideas, project each transparency and discuss the ideas suggested.

11 Take possible ideas, however generated, and ask each member of the group to write down comments for and against and any points of interest each solution suggests.

Staff development

Staff training may be important for the change which is contemplated. This may be a matter of spending a staff development day talking through what you plan, arranging for teachers to attend a short course or organising a short course for everyone in the school. Training may include sending teachers to visit another school where a similar change to the one planned has already been made.

Training is not just something to do before the change starts. Teachers very often need opportunities for further training once they have tried to implement the ideas involved. This may be mainly a matter of talking together about what they are finding and of observing each other and making suggestions. It may be a good idea where the change is in a particular subject area to free the postholder for that subject to coach colleagues in the new ways of working.

Thompson and Sharp (1994 : 91) suggest that it is important to assess learners' needs in relation to the particular change being planned. They suggest a questionnaire asking for 'general information on what areas of information and skills individual staff members feel they need training by providing a list of types of information and specific skills which informants can choose'.

Bradley *et al.* (1994 : 235) state, 'The first lesson is that INSET activities succeed if they are learner-centred, when the learner sees the task as appropriate, finds the activities enjoyable and also finds them underpinned by an element of exploration and problem-solving.'

Implementing change

Fullan and Stiegelbauer (1991 : 47–8) suggest that there are three broad phases to the change process:

Phase 1 – variously labelled initiation, mobilisation, or adoption – consists of the process that leads up to and includes a decision to adopt or proceed with a change.

Phase 2 – implementation or initial use (usually the first two or three years of use) – involves the experiences of attempting to put an idea into practice.

Phase 3 – called continuation, incorporation, routinisation or institutionalisation – refers to whether the change gets built in as an ongoing part of the system or disappears by way of a decision to discard or through attrition.

Once a decision has been made about change, arrangements have to be made about putting it into practice. It is important at this stage to consider whether there are people who should be informed about what is proposed. Do the parents need to know about it? Have the governors been involved, consulted or informed about what is planned? Are there implications for any schools from which you receive children or the secondary schools to which the children will eventually attend? What should the children be told?

Decisions need to made about who will actually introduce the change and the point at which it will begin. Some changes will affect the whole school and others only a part of it.

Once the change process has started it will be important to see that teachers are supported and encouraged. There often comes a low point after about half a term when things do not seem to be working and this is depressing for teachers who may need encouragement to go on and win through to a stage when they feel that they are succeeding. It is helpful if teachers are in the habit of supporting and helping each other and talk together about what they are finding.

Change is only successful if it persists past the early stages and becomes part of the school's normal way of working. This means that the support for teachers and the encouragement must persist until the change becomes accepted as the usual practice. Hopkins (1993 : 9) warns of the way change can be lost. 'Often the working group continues for a while, but eventually it fragments, or another priority is found for them to focus on. The change circles back on itself and nothing much is achieved – so we start something new.'

Stoll and Fink (1996 : 92–7) list norms which underpin successful change:

- Shared goals – we know where we are going.
- Responsibility for success – we must succeed.
- Collegiality – we're working on this together.
- Continuous improvement – we can get better.
- Lifelong learning – learning is for everyone.
- Risk-taking – we learn by trying something new.
- Support – there's always someone there to help.
- Mutual respect – everyone has something to offer.
- Openness – we can discuss our differences.
- Celebration and humour – we feel good about ourselves.

Evaluation

Evaluation will be discussed in detail in Chapter 12. Here it may be said that it is important to evaluate a change in a formal way after it has been running for a period. Evaluation should be planned from the beginning so that information can be collected as the change proceeds. Success criteria should be defined at this stage and wherever possible they should relate to children's achievement. For example, if the change contemplated is an increase in the amount of interactive whole-class teaching in mathematics, then the success criteria might be:

- the amount of whole-class and group interactive mathematics teaching has increased;
- there is an improvement in the mathematics SATs results.

It may be necessary to express these as more specific targets. For example, the increase in whole-class and group interactive teaching needs to be stated in terms of there being a period every day when this takes place in each class. The improvement in the SATs results may need to be expressed in terms of the proportion of children reaching a certain level.

The evaluation process should involve several ways of assessing what has happened. It may include assessing the work of the children involved before the change starts and after a period of change. There may be discussion with the children about their experience of the change, and with older ones, a questionnaire may yield interesting information. Teachers need to discuss their experience and it may be helpful to plan for people to keep a diary of what happens as the change proceeds. It should then be someone's responsibility to collect all these data and report upon them to the whole staff.

Any in-service training involved in the change process also needs to be evaluated. Thompson and Sharp (1994 : 95) suggest that schools need to ask 'What are we evaluating this in-service training for?' and they go on to suggest the answers:

> The purposes of evaluation are usually to give a critical comment on the conduct and methods of delivery of the training events themselves (course evaluation); to find out if the participants have learned something new which is now informing their practice (output evaluation) and to assess how far in-service training was related to actual changes in school life. This last needs a much longer time period over which to assess change.

Problems of change

We have already seen that there are problems arising because the change may challenge teachers' values and beliefs. There are also other problems. Where a school is in difficulties, perhaps having received a poor Ofsted report or becoming unpopular with parents, people may feel too dispirited to want to change anything and may wish to retreat into known practice in the hope that this will turn the tide. They will also probably suggest many solutions which are the responsibility of someone else, such as the local authority or the parents, and avoid taking responsibility themselves for the problems.

Another type of school where a head may find it difficult to get teachers to change is one which is working in a limited way but satisfying the parents because they recognise what is happening as similar to their own experience of school. In both these cases people may put their energy into defending what is currently happening rather than looking for new solutions to their problems.

Another problem is the status of teachers. A teacher who is senior in service may find it difficult to change, not only because change becomes more difficult as we get older but because it may seem an admission that previous work was unsatisfactory. It may be possible to talk to such a person using the fact that seniority makes the example he or she sets very important.

Change may also generate conflict between those teachers who agree with what is being planned and those who disagree. In some circumstances it may be possible to let both groups proceed in their own ways on the basis that they compare results after a period.

Thompson and Sharp (1994 : 85) remind us that 'whilst understanding and expectation may change quickly, as they are intellectual processes, behaviour changes are much slower and are achieved by a series of incremental steps which must be continually encouraged, at least in the early stages'. They also note that it is important that teachers do not feel threatened by change: 'it is likely that the more they feel threatened by the new developments the more their resistance will harden' (p.90).

Hopkins *et al*. (1997 : 75) note that:

The existing internal conditions within the school will make success or failure more or less likely. The reason we need organisational settings in schools which support teachers and students in the process of change is that the experience of change is individually threatening and disconcerting.

Dos and don'ts of change

Fullan and Stiegelbauer (1991 : 106–7) list the following dos and don'ts of change for headteachers:

1 Do not assume that your version of what the change should be is the one that should be implemented.
2 Assume that any significant innovation, if it is to result in change, requires individual implementers to work out their own meaning.
3 Assume that conflict and disagreement are not only inevitable but fundamental to successful change.
4 Assume that most people need pressure to change (even in directions that they desire).
5 Assume that effective change takes time.
6 Do not assume that the reason for lack of implementation is outright rejection of the values embodied in the change, or hard-core resistance to all change.
7 Do not expect all or even most people or groups to change.
8 Assume that you will need a plan that is based on the above assumptions and addresses the factors known to affect implementation.
9 Assume that no amount of knowledge will ever make it totally clear what action should be taken.
10 Assume that changing the culture of institutions is the real agenda, not implementing single innovations.

10

PROFESSIONAL DEVELOPMENT

If schools are to develop, it is essential that the development of staff is taken seriously. Teachers need to be continuously reflecting on and developing their work, not only because change keeps coming from outside, but because knowledge is continuously changing and developing, and no school or teacher can afford to stand still.

Fullan (1992 : 111) describes staff development as 'the sum total of formal and informal learning experiences accumulated across one's career. The agenda then is to work continuously on the spirit and practice of lifelong learning for all teachers.'

Rudduck (1991 : 110) defines professional development as follows:

> Professional development is about the capacity of a teacher to remain curious about the classroom; to identify significant concerns in the process of teaching and learning; to value and seek dialogue with experienced colleagues as support in the analysis of situations; and to adjust patterns of classroom action in the light of new understandings.

Calderhead (1994 : 80) makes the point that teaching is professional because 'teachers possess a body of knowledge acquired through training and experience'. Dean (1991) suggests that one would expect a professional person to have the skill to stand back from current situations and see them in perspective. The process of reflection is important in a teacher's development and effective schools try to encourage it. Hopkins (1993 : 16) says, 'Reflection is the essential building block of professional confidence . . . but reflection is of little use unless it leads to action.'

Nias *et al.* (1992 : 72) stress the importance of the leadership of the headteacher in professional development in their study of primary schools:

> Headteachers demonstrated their personal commitment to learning by actively pursuing their own education, by talking to staff about what they were learning and by showing their willingness to learn. At the same time their example carried two other messages for their

schools; that the professional development of individuals could benefit everyone and that staff members could contribute to and assist one another's learning.

In other words, both teachers and heads saw professional learning as the key to the development of the curriculum and as the main way to improve the quality of the children's education.

Professional development needs to be part of the culture of the developing school. The development of the individual teacher leads to the development of the school as a whole. Although the major emphasis needs to be on the development of teachers, the development of support staff should not be forgotten. The school may be able to run its own in-service development programme for classroom assistants and some authorities also provide courses for this group.

Mortimore *et al*. (1988 : 224) found that:

> Where heads stated that they encouraged and permitted class teachers to go on courses in school time as frequently as they wished, this was associated with poorer progress. In contrast, in schools where teachers were encouraged to go on a course for 'a good reason' there was a positive impact.

This will have changed with the coming of LMS, since schools cannot now afford to let teachers go to any course they wish to attend in school time.

Campbell and Neill (1994) studied the way primary school teachers used their time. They took a very broad definition of professional development which included staff meetings and reading journals, travel to courses, the courses themselves, reading curriculum documents, as well as INSET days. They found that, on average, teachers spent 7.2 hours a week on these activities.

Coulson (1986) stresses the importance of teachers having good self-knowledge as a background to their development. Eraut (1997 : 41) develops this idea:

> Personal knowledge is partly tacit and partly apprehended. A significant consequence of this is that people are not aware of everything they know and only partly aware of their own cognitive frameworks. Hence their personal knowledge is not fully under their own critical control and they should not be confident of its validity.

Teachers are more likely to develop this kind of self-knowledge if they are in the habit of talking about their work and their approaches to it in an open way. Schools with a good collaborative culture foster self-knowledge and encourage reflection. Nias *et al*. (1992 : 78) noted that some teachers in their study 'found an inherent satisfaction in learning, an excitement which became a motivating factor in itself. This was particularly the case when they were aware of belonging to a community of learners.'

Little (1986 : 333) makes a similar point about the American schools she studied:

> In the elementary school selected as 'high success, high involvement' it was difficult to encounter teachers when they were not engaged in some discussion about classroom practice. . . . By contrast, in the less successful schools teachers were likely to report that they restricted formal meetings to administrative business and were likely to consider the faculty lounge off limits to serious topics.

Alexander *et al.* (1989) reported that teachers in their sample said that the main influence on their practice came from colleagues. This could be positive or negative. The school in which a teacher works is an important influence on his or her self-image, way of thinking about the work and ability to cope with change and development.

Fullan (1992 : 23) suggests that 'Since implementation [of change] involves learning to do something new, it follows that schools that foster a learning orientation among their staff as well as their students are more likely to bring about improvements.'

Moore (1988) suggests that teacher learning opportunities should:

- collaborative, involving participants in diagnosing needs, decision making, designing, implementing and evaluating staff development;
- help learners to achieve self-direction and be able to define their own objectives, using professional content to meet their needs;
- capitalise on learners' experiences, using them as a starting point;
- foster participation, with learners helping to decide learning methods and structure the learning environment;
- cultivate critical, reflective thinking, helping learners examine cultural and organisational assumptions as well as their own practice;
- foster learning for action, with opportunities for decision making and strategy planning;
- encourage problem-posing and problem-solving, as closely connected as possible to learner's real problems;
- have a climate of respect, with interchangeable facilitators and participants, opportunities for small-group interaction, comfortable furniture and, we would add, food!

Professional development policy

Every school needs a policy for professional development. Such a policy might include the following:

- *Overall philosophy and attitudes towards professional development* This section might include a statement that it is the policy of the school to provide for the learning and development of all its staff.
- *The people whom the policy concerns* Professional development should concern all staff, non-teaching as well as teaching staff and including the head-teacher.
- *The possible professional development activities* The policy should make it clear that there are many activities in which staff may be involved which lead to their development as well as those which are clearly in-service activities. It may also be a good idea to list those such as appraisal and observation of other teachers at work which may give rise to concern.
- *Responsibility for professional development* Various people have responsibility for professional development. The headteacher and deputy, coordinators and anyone else in a leadership role is responsible for seeing that colleagues develop in their work. There should also be someone with overall responsibility for professional development. In a small school this will inevitably be the headteacher, but in a larger school a more senior teacher may take on this task. It will also be necessary from time to time to have someone responsible for the induction and development of newly qualified teachers. Teachers new to the staff may require induction into the ways of the school. There may also be a case in a large school for a staff team to oversee professional development.
- *The way needs will be assessed* Needs assessment is an important part of the programme and staff must know what opportunities they will have to make their needs clear.
- *The part played by appraisal* Appraisal is an important way of assessing the needs of staff as well as contributing to their development through discussion.
- *Provision for induction and mentoring* New members of staff, however experienced, benefit from induction into the school culture and routines. Newly qualified teachers need mentoring as well as induction and further training.
- *Provision for management training* Every school should provide management training for its senior staff and for other teachers who see themselves eventually moving into management posts. Much of this may be by offering opportunities for leadership and discussing what is involved and how best to undertake the work.
- *The way in which provision for individuals is built up* Professional development is something which should be discussed regularly with individuals, usually as part of the appraisal process. The policy ought also to make a statement about opportunities for career interviews.
- *The arrangements for professional portfolios* A school should help teachers by keeping a record of their work and development. It is useful to ask each teacher to provide a statement annually of groups taught, extra-curricular

activities undertaken, contributions to the school as a whole and any involvement in courses or other professional development activities.

Needs assessment

Schools should assess needs annually. It is common to feel in a small school, in particular, that this can be undertaken informally but needs may be missed if there is not a formal pattern of needs assessment.

Kerwood and Clements (1986 : 227) make the following points about needs assessment:

> The message the teachers should receive is that it is their own perception of their needs which is the starting point; that they are being trusted to formulate their own problems; that they are being valued as the principal resource, that they are being given the power to manage their own learning and develop their own solutions. In short, the message is one of empowerment. . . . The confidence that this realisation brings to the staff enables them to look for expert and theoretical help from outside when they need it, and to be more open in the way they approach their work and their problems, evaluating, appraising and consulting one another and sharing ideas, successes and failures.

Kydd et al. (1997 : 131) note that 'Staff development can be threatening because it involves revealing a "gap" between present and required or desired performance.' It is therefore important that needs assessment is handled sensitively, with emphasis on development not remediation. The authors also stress that 'staff development must view holistically the personal and professional lives of teachers as individuals'.

There are three areas in which needs can be identified. People may say what they think they need. Needs can be deduced from various kinds of documentation and they can be identified by observation, including the following techniques:

- critical incidents or problems can be used as starting points;
- teachers and other staff can be given questionnaires to help them identify their needs;
- teachers and other staff can be interviewed, perhaps using a questionnaire as a starting point;
- teachers and other staff can be observed at work;
- the school development plan can be studied. Certain teachers may be asked to undertake courses in order to help the school meet targets;
- discussion of job descriptions as part of the appraisal process may clarify particular needs;

- teachers new to the school may need training in particular areas as part of the school's development;
- a staff conference may be held;
- appraisal discussions which look at career prospects may give rise to certain needs, such as management training;
- some teachers will need management training to deal with tasks in their particular role.

The development programme

Once needs have been identified the programme can be built up. In the event it is unlikely that everyone's needs can be met and the ideas which have been put forward need to be put in priority order. The programme will not only be limited by time but by the costs of sending people to courses and supply cover. MacGilchrist *et al.* (1995 : 215) point out that 'supply cover will be necessary not just for release to work alongside others and to attend in-service training sessions but also to enable individuals and teams of teachers to fulfil their leadership and management responsibilities'.

The starting point for the programme is to state its objectives in a form that can be monitored and assessed. Parts of the programme will be formal in-service activities and other parts will be informal ways of helping people to develop, such as visits to other schools, staff discussion about ways of teaching, and so on.

The next stage is to assess the time available for the programme. Schools will have in-service days but some assessment should be made of other time available and ways of increasing this may need to be considered. Using supply cover is an obvious way and the headteacher, who is not normally involved with a class, may be willing to do some extra teaching to release colleagues to work with each other, observe each other, address a particular aspect of a task for the school or attend a course. Teachers may also be willing to devote time after school to development work.

The formal parts of the programme need to be planned in some detail and consideration given at the planning stage to the ways in which they will be evaluated. Some parts of the programme will apply to everyone. Other parts will be for particular individuals. The formal programme will include attendance at external courses as well as in-service activities in school.

The informal programme

A wide variety of activities offer opportunities for development. For example:

- discussing problems in a small group;
- action research with a small group of teachers investigating a particular aspect of teaching and learning;

- experiencing a job-exchange or job-shadowing;
- having the opportunity to lead a development or in-service activity;
- taking part in a working party dealing with work needed by the school;
- observing another teacher at work and discussing what happened;
- team teaching with another teacher;
- visiting another school to see particular work in action and reporting back to colleagues on findings;
- reading a particular book and reporting on it to colleagues;
- being involved in helping to write a school policy or scheme of work;
- receiving and using advice from a subject coordinator, the head or deputy or an external source;
- coaching in a particular way of teaching;
- keeping a diary of development and discussing this with a colleague;
- getting feedback from children on the effectiveness of a particular lesson or lessons.

Evaluation

We have already noted that evaluation of the development programme should be planned at the beginning and success criteria must be defined. All the formal activities need to be evaluated in a formal way, perhaps using questionnaires, interviewing or both and it is helpful to find a way of assessing the value to individuals of the informal activities. Questions such as the following, asked at the end of the year, may be useful:

- In what ways do you feel your work has developed during this year?
- What is your evidence for this?
- Which activities have contributed most to this development?
- In what ways would you like to develop your work in the future?
- What activities would be helpful to you in this development?

Bradley (1988) suggests that evaluation of formal professional development activities should involve considering the following:

- Preparation – was the needs assessment adequate? Was there appropriate preparation by the school?
- Planning – were there clear goals and consideration of possible changes of attitude needed?
- Execution – did participants recognise the purpose and value of the activity? Did they enjoy it?
- Follow up – was there encouragement by the school to use the learning the activity had offered?

Evaluation will also be part of the appraisal process, in that it will be an opportunity not only for individuals to discuss their development with a colleague but for teachers to feed back critically their views on the development opportunities they have experienced during the year.

Since teacher development has the main purpose of improving the learning of children, evidence should be sought as to whether this is happening. Are the SATs results improving? Are children scoring more highly in tests of reading and mathematics? Are they more enthusiastic about their work?

Appraisal

All schools are now supposed to be appraising the work of all teachers at regular intervals. In practice, schools are finding it difficult to find the time for this process, since it involves not only an interview of reasonable length but observation of the teacher at work. If an appraisal scheme is to be successful, it requires commitment on the part of the headteacher and staff.

Day *et al*. (1987 : 115) suggest that a teacher asking the question 'What's in it for me?' should be able to answer in the following ways:

1 I should have a clear understanding of my job, how well I am doing it and what is expected of me.
2 I should feel secure in the knowledge that my talents are known, appreciated and exploited and that my weaknesses have been identified and constructive help offered to improve them.
3 I should have discussed my future, including my ambition and career prospects, and have received guidance in achieving those ambitions.
4 I should feel satisfied that all aspects of my work in and around the school have been discussed in a professional way.
5 I should feel happy that everything discussed will be treated in confidence and any written note will be owned by myself and my interviewer alone.

The letter about appraisal sent by the then Secretary of State for Education to Chief Education Officers (DfE 1990) suggests that appraisal schemes should:

- help teachers to identify ways of enhancing their professional skill;
- assist in planning the in-service training and professional development of teachers individually and collectively;
- help individual teachers, their headteachers, governing body and local education authorities (where appropriate) to see where a new or modified assignment would help the professional development of individual teachers and improve their career prospects;
- identify the potential of teachers for career development with the aim of helping them where possible through appropriate in-service training;

- provide help to teachers having difficulty with their performance, through appropriate guidance, counselling and training. Disciplinary and dismissal procedures shall remain quite separate but may need to draw upon relevant information from appraisal records;
- inform those responsible for providing references for teachers;
- enhance the overall management of schools.

Dodd (1991 : 79) notes that appraisal can be a credit or a debit approach and suggests that it is important that the approach is positive and 'values each individual teacher's performance, qualities and potential and serves as a means of providing motivation'. He goes on to say, 'This approach provides each teacher with support and feedback through recognising effective teaching and practice resulting in a perceptive enrichment of provision for all pupils.' He states that in his work as coordinator of Newcastle's teacher appraisal pilot project he found this kind of approach produced positive benefits for schools, teachers and pupils, and that

> It was . . . an important initial task to begin to get teachers to identify the many things that were going well and in which they were being successful. A balance needed to be achieved between success, needs and direction and for each individual teacher. It also meant quite a cultural shock for many now had permission to celebrate success, develop their self-confidence and self-esteem and actually to enjoy the process.
>
> (Dodd 1991 : 77)

Appraisal also provides an opportunity for helping to coordinate the work of the school or a section of the school. It offers the opportunity to guide teachers' work and to influence the thinking of individual teachers towards the overall school vision. It also provides an opportunity for praising what is good and dealing with unsatisfactory elements of performance. Teachers also have an opportunity to ensure that relevant others know about their work and it gives them an opportunity to express any views they may have about the management of the school. Kydd *et al.* (1997 : 6) note that 'Systems such as appraisal serve an important organisational function and are one of the mechanisms by which individuals are socialised into and maintained within the organisation's purposes, values and outcomes.'

Appraisal involves the observation of a teacher's work by an appraiser. This necessitates discussion among the staff and agreement about what is to be observed and when. Teachers are not always skilled as observers and careful consideration should be given to what can be learned from observation. It is also important that the observer is clear about the teacher's intentions in any work observed and that there is discussion about it in terms of what was intended.

Observation should include attention to the relationship of teacher and children, the way the teacher responds to children's contributions to the lesson, the quality of the teacher's exposition and explanations and the questioning which takes place. To what extent do the questions the teacher asks make children think, as distinct from recalling what they have already been taught? What is the pace and timing of the lesson like? Is there a good mixture of approaches and activities? Does what is happening command children's attention? How do the children respond? What is their work like? Is there evidence of progression and development?

Appraisal interviews need careful preparation and it is useful if the person being appraised completes some form of questionnaire or makes a written statement as a preliminary. The appraiser needs to look at all the relevant material in advance and have a clear idea of the plan of the interview which needs to be organised so that the person being appraised does most of the talking and the appraiser listens carefully and receptively, extending what is said where necessary. The plan of the interview should be discussed at the beginning to ensure that the teacher concerned is happy with the plan and has the opportunity to modify it if he or she wishes. The appraiser should summarise at intervals; development and career prospects should be discussed and goals should be agreed. There should be an opportunity for the person being appraised to raise any problems or comment on aspects of the work of the school with which he or she is unhappy. The interview should end with a summary by the appraiser, and a written report on the interview which is confidential to the appraiser and teacher concerned may serve as a permanent record.

Induction of newly qualified teachers

Earley and Kinder (1994 : 1) make the point that 'the experience of the first year is most formative and there is a need to set high expectations and standards when there is the greatest receptiveness'. They point out that induction 'can be seen as the first stage in a comprehensive programme of professional support and development available throughout a teacher's career'.

Induction should be carefully planned but also sufficiently flexible to allow for the needs of individual NQTs. In a secondary school there may be several NQTs arriving at the same time, but this is rare in a primary school. Consequently, the programme tends to be more informal but it is still necessary to think carefully about the ground which should be covered for all new teachers in terms of the school's practices. Too many areas should not be covered at once. It is a good idea to list the topics which need to be covered by all new teachers, not only NQTs. These might include such things as the school vision and values, school policies, schemes of work, the role of coordinators, practices in record keeping and assessment, school rules and arrangements for dealing with children who misbehave, arrangements for assemblies, playtime and dinner duties, fire drill, how to acquire new stock, and so on.

Most schools arrange for someone to act as a mentor to a newly qualified teacher. According to Earley and Kinder (1994) this may be a senior member of staff, the headteacher or a recently qualified teacher. In the last case there will be a need for someone more senior to be involved as well so that some assessment can be made of the NQT's progress. The mentor's role might include giving classroom support, perhaps working alongside the teacher and planning some work together, observing the NQT in the classroom and offering observations, providing information about the school systems, organising the induction programme and keeping an eye on the welfare of the new teacher.

Teachers at the beginning of their careers are working out what their teaching style will be. They need the opportunity to observe skilled and experienced teachers at work. Observation of other teachers in the same school or in neighbouring schools is valuable, especially if there is a chance to discuss with the teacher what has been observed.

Newly qualified teachers may also have the opportunity to take part in LEA-organised programmes for new teachers and these may not only be helpful but offer an opportunity to talk with other teachers at the same stage.

The induction programme should incorporate opportunities and encouragement for the teacher to reflect on practice. This is an important element in developing work and important as a practice for future development.

Professional records

A school should have records of the work of teachers and their contribution to the life of the school that can furnish information for any reports on their work which are required when they seek promotion or in disciplinary cases. These should include a record of professional development activities.

Teachers also need their own professional records. Hall (1997 : 171) suggests that each teacher should keep a 'professional development portfolio' which he describes as 'a collection of material, made by a professional, that records, and reflects on, key events and processes in that professional's career'. He goes on to claim that 'by reflecting on the achievement of the past a portfolio can boost a professional's confidence and alter the way he or she approaches the future. People can become more organised and structured in their work.' He also suggests that 'It could form the basis for a rational system of appraisal. It would focus the appraisal process on the individual's progress and needs and go some way to remove the anxiety that currently exists' (p.172).

Effective staff development

Wideen (1987) summarises research on successful staff development. It involves paying attention to the contexts in which teachers are working, addresses issues of teacher participation and collaboration, has continuity over time and is reflective and analytical.

> Participants, teachers and administrators, are seldom encouraged to stand back and think seriously about what they do or might be doing. . . . Strong programmes of staff development not only account for these activities but build them into programmes. Time is set aside for rigorous examination of what has happened and is happening. Individual and group introspection is encouraged.
>
> (Wideen 1987 : 33)

West (1994 : 151) makes some further points:

- Effective staff development starts from *where the teacher is*, though informed by a view of where he or she is going. It is a 'building from' rather than a 'deficit' approach.
- Effective staff development involves teachers recognising that they can and do learn 'on the job' – the classroom is an important development centre for teachers as well as pupils.
- During the development process, feedback is available to stimulate and to reassure teachers who are experimenting with new behaviour.
- The best opportunities for staff development relate to those activities which teachers find meaningful and satisfying.

11

PARENTS, GOVERNORS AND THE COMMUNITY

Parents

Traditional involvement of parents

Munn (1993 : 1) suggests that there are three aspects to the traditional way in which schools have involved parents:

- it has largely concerned the well-being of the parents' own child;
- it has been to support the largely taken-for-granted value system of the school;
- collective action, such as through parents' or parent–teacher associations, has been largely concerned with fund-raising, or transmitting information, and has not usually challenged the school's way of doing things.

Atkin *et al.* (1988 : 46) note that 'Schools filter and screen opportunities for parents to see the life and work of the school, often in a limiting way. Schools underestimate how much this happens and its consequences.' Parents are familiar with individual teachers, school routines, and recurring events in the school calendar. They may not be familiar with the school's educational philosophy and educational policies, the curriculum and teaching strategies. They may conceptualise teaching 'as formal, planned and systematic instruction' (p.73). 'School is where children sit and learn. What is learned through play is rarely articulated' (p.35).

Recent changes have made it necessary to involve parents much more in what the school is about. Schools are more evidently accountable to parents, among others, and are dependent for their income on parents choosing the school for their children. It has also become increasingly clear that children whose parents support them in school and are prepared to contribute to their learning are more likely to succeed in their school work. Parents therefore need to know and become committed to the values of the school. They must be aware of the curriculum the school is following and how the teaching is carried out. They also need opportunities to contribute from their own knowledge of their children. Teachers should think about how parents know what is happening in the school, how their children are learning and the contribution they can make.

Earley (1994 : 90) reports the following comment from a chair of governors:

> Very often schools are like little islands in the middle of their communities. They often don't know what the temperature is outside; how parents see the school and the difficulties they have in understanding what the children are being taught and why in that way. We get to talk to lots of them outside in other situations.

The first reaction to this comment by people in primary schools is likely to be that it is an exaggeration. Most primary schools see a lot of their parents and in these days of competition for pupils are likely to take a lot of care to keep them happy.

However, there is research which suggests that although schools see a lot of parents, they could do more to explain what they are doing. Tizard *et al.* (1988), in their study of young children in the inner city, found that much of what parents knew about what was happening in school was gleaned from looking at their children's work, rather than from teachers. Atkin *et al.* (1988) had a similar finding, revealing a small but significant number of parents who described understandings which had emerged from the process of asking children to explain work to them.

Tizard *et al.* (1988) found that parents were not given much information about how their child was doing relative to other children. Teachers were quite likely to have told parents that their child was doing well when in fact the child was not. Only 20 per cent of parents had been given an indication that their child was having difficulties when testing showed that a much larger proportion were in this category. Similarly only 12 per cent of parents had been told that their child posed behaviour problems whereas the teachers reckoned that there were 26 per cent who posed problems.

They also found that teachers had negative views of black parents while the study showed that black parents actually did more to help their children with school work than white parents.

Another area where they found that schools could do more to inform parents was over curriculum plans, on which the authors comment:

> We think there is a strong case for informing parents of the curriculum plans for the year, and also enlisting their help in assessment at the end of the year. They would be an important source of information about their child's reading habits, interests, ability to use mathematics in a practical situation and so on.
>
> (Tizard *et al.* 1988 : 175)

Current involvement of parents

These studies were done some time ago and there have been many changes and developments since then. However, some of the findings are still likely to be true in some schools. In others much is being done to involve parents. Webb and Vulliamy (1996 : 122–3) comment about schools in their study:

> We found that most schools were expanding the range of ways in which parents were involved in the life of the school. These included: encouraging volunteer helpers in the school library, the classroom and on school visits, organising meetings and workshops, organising National Curriculum meetings and workshops, setting up paired reading schemes, holding painting and repairing weekends, evenings of family entertainment and fund-raising schemes.
>
> They were producing more detailed school brochures, school newsletters, leaflets on curriculum initiatives, school calendars, displays specifically for parents, pupil homework diaries and the involvement of parents in their children's record of achievement.

Schools are making this kind of effort to involve parents not only as part of marketing the school but because headteachers and teachers know that when home and school work together the children make better progress. This was a finding of research by Douglas as far back as 1964 and there have been many studies since which confirm his findings in various ways. Bastiani (1993 : 103) notes that:

> These successful schools go well beyond the basic legal requirements to develop effective two-way communication, are accessible in a variety of ways and at all reasonable times, work hard to find ways in which parents can encourage and support their children and provide them with practical help and above all, build a sense of shared identity and common purpose.

Atkin *et al.* (1988 : 7) suggest that when parents

- understand what the school is trying to do;
- identify with its main goals and support its efforts;
- understand something of their role as educators;
- take an active interest in, and provide support for their children's school work;

then the effects can be both dramatic and long-lasting.

Mortimore *et al.* (1988 : 226) found a beneficial effect where parents helped in the classrooms and with visits and where there were progress meetings and a parents' room: 'Where it was the practice for parents to call in at any time to see the head [this] was also associated with progress.'

Who is a parent?

One of the problems for schools today which was much rarer in the past is that children can have more than two 'parents'. Dean (1995b : 207) makes the following comment:

> Under the Children's Act 1992, parents of a dissolved partnership may seek from the courts parental rights. When these are granted he or she must be given access to school reports, invited to school functions and in all respects be treated as equal with the partner who is parenting. When a partner has not been granted these rights, the school may be in breach of the law in communicating with that partner unless the other partner specifically requests it. Divorced parents usually have equal rights. The new partner only has rights if the child is legally adopted. In such a case the new parents may well supersede the birthright parents. The school needs to be clear about any child where there has been separation.

Parents as teachers

Topping and Wolfendale (1985) point out that if children are learning all the time, parents and other adults are, in effect, teaching all the time. They are acting as role models and the school can assist them in ways which help the learning of their children. The authors set out the ways in which teachers and parents contribute to the child's learning:

> Teachers bring knowledge of child development and theories of learning and teaching and have the advantage of an accumulating store of professional wisdom as the backcloth to their practice. They can appraise individual differences in learning receptivity, rate of learning etc. and can match each child's learning needs to the provision on offer.
>
> Parents contribute their life experiences as well as accumulating knowledge of their own child's (or children's) development and individual characteristics and have the advantage of experiencing minute-by-minute child contact in a variety of situations. They, too, can appraise their child's learning responsiveness; they can make predictions as to outcomes and make a match between what the child needs . . . with whatever resources and support the home and family have to offer.
>
> (Topping and Wolfendale 1985 : 12)

These writers and other contributors to their book go on to describe work in various schools in which parents became involved in helping their children in learning to read, either by hearing them read on a regular basis or by using paired reading where parents and child read aloud together. The schools working in this way have spent time training parents in the techniques required and making sure they know what to do when a child hesitates over a word or makes a mistake. The overall effect of this work was very positive, with children who were helped by their parents making much better progress than children not included in the schemes, even when the former came from homes where 'the language atmosphere was apparently unfavourable' (p.45).

Sullivan (1991) describes prepared reading, where parent and child discuss a book together and the parent then reads a passage with the child following. The child then reads the same passage with the parent prompting where necessary.

Parents' and teachers' views of each other

Parents and teachers tend to have stereotypes of each other, largely formed in the parents' case by their own experience of school. This may make some parents very hesitant about coming to the school. They may see teachers as frightening, or as friends or as rather underpaid employees. Teachers for their part often have stereotypes about parents and assume that working-class parents are not particularly interested in their children's education, especially if they do not, for one reason or another, come into the school very often. Tizard *et al.* (1988) found that there were very few parents who were not interested in their children's education. Teachers also often have a stereotyped view of 'pushy middle-class parents' who appear to expect the impossible. In practice such parents may be rather unsure of themselves. Teachers are also influenced in their views of parents by their own experience in that role themselves. Parents are a considerable resource to the school if teachers give them the chance to participate in their children's education.

Ethnic minority parents

Tomlinson and Hutchinson (1991) found that the contact with parents in schools where there were large numbers of Bangladeshi children coming from homes where English was not spoken was very limited. This was made more difficult by the fact that half of the mothers and a fifth of the fathers had had no schooling at all and were unable to read and write. Very few schools had strategies to overcome these problems and teachers tended to be patronising. Parents did not receive the level of information about their children's progress that they wanted. Twenty months after the advent of the National Curriculum 90 per cent of the mothers and 40 per cent of the fathers knew nothing about it.

Tomlinson (1993 : 144) makes the following point about schools with many children from ethnic minorities:

> There is evidence that teachers are still not well informed about the lives, backgrounds, expectations and desires of ethnic minority parents and are still willing to stereotype such families as 'problems'. Ethnic minority parents are less likely than white parents to be involved in the day-to-day school activities and to be represented on governing bodies.

Tomlinson also found that while ethnic minority parents often have high hopes for their children, 'teacher expectations of pupils whose backgrounds, culture and language they did not understand have been consistently low and this has persisted as a generation of British-born young ethnic minority pupils have entered school' (p.133).

Schools with this kind of problem need to consider carefully ways in which they can communicate with parents, particularly those whose knowledge of English is limited. It may be possible to translate communications if there are not too many different languages spoken by parents. Older children in particular play a valuable part in communicating information to their parents about what they are doing in school, and the school can encourage this.

Marketing the school

Most schools are in competition for children and consequently for the money that they bring, and therefore need to take marketing the school seriously.

Barnes (1993 : 1–2) describes marketing in education as follows:

> It is a philosophy or approach to providing education services which is essentially consumer oriented; it involves identifying needs and wants of specified clients, designing (with due regard to prevailing educational and professional standards and ethos) appropriate education services to satisfy those needs and wants, communicating the existence of the education service to clients and delivering the desired product to them.

He suggests that schools should think in terms of 'segmentation', by which he means 'the identification of the numerous sub groups which make up the mass market' (p.8). This makes it possible to target specific audiences. This will be particularly necessary when a school serves an area which is socially or racially mixed.

Bagley et al. (1997 : 258) suggest that 'For marketing to be effective, schools need to have a clear view of what parents think, how they make decisions and what they look for in a school. It also requires schools to have effective means of acting on this knowledge and understanding.'

The authors surveyed a range of schools, looking at their marketing activities. They found a tendency for schools to be more responsive to middle-class parents and also that there was a considerable reliance on ad hoc feedback.

James and Phillips (1997) collected data on marketing from eleven schools, of which three were grant-maintained primary schools. They found that all the schools in their survey had a good understanding of what they offered their customers and 'almost all the schools realised that there was a need to high-light various aspects of their provision' (p.276). However, none of the schools described the services they offered in terms of the benefits and

In all schools, including the private schools, there was an:

- unclear recognition of market segments;
- absence of data on market needs;
- inadequate marketing links with the recipients.

(James and Phillips 1997 : 277)

They also suggest that it is important for headteachers to market the school to the staff, so that they in turn are good public relations advocates of the school.

Exploring parental opinion

Good public relations involves schools identifying the characteristics of the various groups which make up the school population and this will be necessary in order to set realistic marketing objectives. In the first instance this will be a matter of considering the parents of children in the local environment. It will then be a matter of looking further afield and considering parents whom the school would like to attract. Target audiences might include prospective parents, headteachers and staff of any feeder schools, estate agents, and so on.

Schools need to find ways of tapping the opinions of all these groups and particularly of parents of children currently in the school. Ofsted requires a survey of parental opinion as well as having a meeting of parents with the Registered Inspector. This is often very useful to the school. Some schools use regular surveys to find out how parents are viewing what is happening, perhaps surveying a class at a time. It is as well to consider at the start what will be involved in analysing the questionnaires so that no one is overburdened, and to make it clear to parents that different groups of parents will be sampled at a time. Even in schools where very few of the parents speak English, but where there are older children, it is possible to make a survey by using children in Years 5 and 6 to ask questions of their parents and record the answers. This can also be a good way of ensuring that most parents send in answers, although the questionnaire will have to be rather carefully designed if it is to be administered by children.

Another possibility is to have class meetings or year-group meetings at which the teachers give parents information about curriculum plans for the class or year and talk over ways in which parents could help with this, giving parents a chance to make suggestions as well as providing information. Such a meeting could conclude with a questionnaire, partly about the meeting but including some more general questions.

Discussion with parents needs to be two-way. Parents know their children very well and teachers have something to learn from parents about the children in their class. From this point of view the regular individual meeting with parents is helpful, providing the teacher concerned gives the parents a chance to talk as well as telling them about their child's progress. There is much to be said for the kind of meeting set up in one first school where all parents of new entrants were seen for an in-depth discussion about their children a month after they started school. This had three purposes: to check on factual information, to hear the parents' view of how the child had settled and to listen to what the parents could tell the school about the child.

Parents may also contribute to children's records and assessments in various ways. When the child first enters school it may be helpful to have samples of the child's drawings, possibly tapes of his or her conversation, as well as information from the parent about what the child is able to do.

Communication with parents

Schools need to think carefully about their communication with parents, in terms of both meetings and written communication. This is not easy because the parents of a school may range from graduates to people who are near illiterate and may include parents who do not speak English. Writing or planning meetings for such a wide-ranging audience poses considerable problems. It may also be a good idea to survey what parents think of the communication from time to time.

The school is legally committed to one meeting a year of the parent body and in many schools this is not well attended. Smaller meetings, such as class meetings, may attract more parents, particularly if they are recognised as dealing with the work their children are currently doing. Some schools find sessions where parents undertake some of the tasks their children are experiencing very successful since they involve participation and this tends to arouse greater interest than merely hearing about something. On the other hand, some parents may find these sessions intimidating.

The recent emphasis on results and performance tables tends to give the impression that parents are only interested in this kind of information. Most parents value the human qualities of schools and the happiness of their children. Schools need to remember this in planning their marketing.

Meetings with parents to discuss their child's progress

Undoubtedly the most important meetings are those where individual parents have a chance to talk with the class teacher about their child's work. Teachers must inform parents of where their child has reached in the National Curriculum and the best way of doing this is in a face-to-face interview. These need good planning so that the timetable for talking to each set of parents is strictly adhered to. There should also be a measure of privacy and teachers must record the main points of each meeting so that they can refer back to what was said when they meet the same parents later. It can be helpful if these meetings follow the sending of school reports on each child's progress. Parents then have information to discuss. Sullivan (1991 : 104) notes that 'It is still rare to find these occasions used as a meeting where parent and teacher collaborate about ways and means of working jointly together to bring about improvements in the child's progress.'

Intentions behind reporting are as follows:

• to widen access to information about the school's curriculum plans and objectives for individual children and classes in the case of parents and more generally for the school as a whole;
• to provide parents with the information necessary to support an informed dialogue with the school and with the children themselves about their achievements, progress and future work throughout their school career;
• to encourage partnership between schools and parents by sharing information and explaining its implications;
• to enable a school to report on the overall accomplishments of its children in ways that not only parents but the wider community can appreciate.

Teachers tend to prefer children to see their progress in the light of their own performance, but parents really want to know how the progress of their child compares with others. The National Curriculum assessment makes this clear in terms of the various levels and at the same time shows that for some children the picture can be complex, with their reaching different levels in different subjects.

These meetings should include discussion about what the teacher intends to do to help the child and how the parents can help. Research suggests that teachers have a tendency to tell parents what not to do rather than what to do and it is important to keep the conversation positive.

Written communication

Written communication needs to be clear and friendly without jargon. It is salutary to remember that what is the normal language for teachers discussing their work may well be jargon to a parent. Sentences should be short and uncomplicated. The appearance of communications is important. They should be easy to read, well spaced with good use of headings to direct the eye. There is no excuse in these days of word processors for poor reproduction of written communication. There should as far as possible be translations where necessary for parents who speak other languages, though where the school includes children from many different language backgrounds this may be near impossible. Many schools produce newsletters for parents; these tend to contain information about fund-raising activities and so on. They offer good opportunities for communicating about the curriculum and current work, and on how parents can help with projects. There is a case for class newsletters dealing with the work of the class and the contribution parents can make.

People will be more likely to attend to messages that are:

- written to them personally;
- clearly of use to them;
- in language that they can easily understand which is free of jargon;
- well laid-out so that what is important can clearly be seen;
- short enough to be read by busy parents;
- in tune with their own views and values.

School reports

A particularly important communication is the school report. Schools now have to provide a written report on each child's progress which states the stage the child has reached in the National Curriculum and also gives information about other areas of work and work skills, behaviour, attitudes and any problems. It must also give information about the average class performance. Teachers have the difficult task of writing reports which are honest yet encouraging. Schools need to have a very clear policy on the criteria which are used to describe each child's progress and ensure that this information is equally clear to parents. It is a good idea to discuss the form of reports with parents from time to time to see if the report form used is meeting their need for information about their children's progress.

Parents visiting or phoning the school

Another area of communication is the reception parents receive when they come to the school or phone. Is the main entrance clearly marked? It can be difficult to find in some older schools and new parents may find themselves in a classroom while looking for the way in. Is the teacher helpful in this circumstance? Is the secretary helpful and friendly when a parent comes into the school or phones?

Home visits

Teachers are busy people, and in any case have a life outside school. Nevertheless, any teacher who can find the time to visit parents at home will be amply rewarded, usually by the welcome he or she will receive, but also by the knowledge that this activity gives about the child and by the relationship it builds with the parents.

Marketing objectives

The first task in marketing is to set clear and detailed objectives. Oxley (1987) suggests that the first objective might be to make the organisation well known and understood. Another objective might be to attract positive comment in the local press. A school should also aim to ensure that parents know the work which will be taking place in their child's class in the coming year. The school could also be made more user friendly to visitors.

Learning to deal with parents

Teachers need help and support in their contacts with parents, especially when they are new in teaching. This is not something that initial training usually encompasses. The teachers in the Tizard study (1988) who were hesitant about giving parents information that their children were not doing very well needed some help in thinking how to put this kind of view across in a way that was not too upsetting and which enlisted the parent's help rather than antagonising him or her. It can be helpful to have a staff discussion about situations which teachers have found difficult in discussing with parents, thinking out ways of meeting these difficulties and perhaps providing role-play situations, particularly for inexperienced teachers.

Teachers also need to consider the training of parents helping in the classroom or around the school. It may be a good idea to have an in-service day involving some parents to consider the school's involvement of parents in the work of the school.

Parents helping in the school

Parents in many schools are playing an important part in the work of the school, helping in various ways both in the classrooms and about the school. This requires careful planning and it is important that teachers working with parents in the classroom plan carefully for the work of parents and any other support they may have. Neville Bennett and Kell (1989) studied four-year-olds in infant classes and in the process examined what parents and other helpers were doing. They found that in many cases the helpers were left to their own devices and in some cases were not supporting the teacher very well.

A particular problem about parents helping in the school is how such parents are chosen. Does the school accept all who volunteer? If some parents are chosen and not others, this can lead to bitterness and resentment. Teachers may not want some parents on the grounds that they are not very literate or are inclined to take over. The parent who is not very literate may learn a good deal from the experience of being in the school and tasks should be selected which individuals can do. The parent who is inclined to take over can be kept in check if the teacher with whom he or she is working is clear about what is required.

In many areas there are parents who have special knowledge and skills which would be of use to the school, and every effort should be made to use their talents. Bilingual parents, in particular, will be of considerable value both in translating communications to other parents and in translating and recording material into the home language of children who are learning English, and then working with them to translate the story back into English.

Schools also have to come to some conclusions about how parents working in the school are to be treated. What will they do at break times? Will they be allowed to use the staff room and, if so, does this place too much constraint on the teachers? It is important to impress on parents helping in school the need for confidentiality about what they see and hear; this will be particularly important if they enter the staff room. It should also be ensured that parents working in the school are covered by the school's insurance.

A further consideration is whether parent helpers should be trained, and what form this training should take. To some extent this depends upon the role the school expects them to play. If they are to help in the classroom, then there is much to be said for spending time explaining the way teaching is carried out and the contribution the parents can make. Similarly, if parents are to hear reading or play number games with children, they need to be informed about what to do if the child does not recognise a word or forgets the number fact he or she needs for the next stage in a game.

Assessing parental involvement

Schools need to evaluate their work with parents, and the following statements may help with this. A staff can consider whether each statement is true of the involvement parents have in their school.

- Parents know what the school is aiming at and how teachers are setting out to achieve it.
- Every effort is made to involve parents as soon as their child joins the school.
- All parents are known by their child's class teacher.
- Parents have many opportunities to make judgments about the standards of learning and teaching.

- All parents feel welcome in the school and are treated as partners in their children's education.
- Parents are kept fully informed about their child's progress, potential and achievement.
- All parents have regular and adequate opportunities to talk over their child's progress and any difficulties he or she is encountering.
- Teachers listen to parents, take note of their views of their child's progress and learn from their knowledge of their child.
- All teachers prepare adequately for meetings with parents and make notes of important points from these meetings.
- Parents are made to feel that they have a contribution to make to their child's education which is recognised and appreciated by the school.
- Inexperienced teachers are trained for their work with parents and supported in it until they feel competent.
- Parents are involved in the work of the school and help in a variety of ways. Teachers give clear guidance to parent helpers.
- The school uses every kind of parent skill to enrich the curriculum and the experience of the children.
- There are parent/teacher activities to suit all kinds of people and every effort is made to involve reluctant parents.
- Parents are made aware of the channels of communication with the governors which are open to them through the parent governors.

Governors

The responsibilities of governors

The DfEE booklet *School Governors: A Guide to the Law* (1997b : 15) lists the following responsibilities for governors:

- deciding (with the head and the LEA if appropriate) the aims and policies of the school, and how the standards of education can be improved;
- deciding the conduct of the school – that is, how in general terms it should be run;
- helping to draw up (with the head and staff) the school development plan;
- deciding (taking account of anything in the LMS scheme and any powers they may pass to the head) how to spend the school's budget;
- making sure that the National Curriculum and religious education are taught and reporting on National Curriculum assessments and examination results;
- selecting the head and deputy head;

- appointing, promoting, supporting and disciplining other staff in consultation with the head;
- acting as a link between the local community and the school; and
- drawing up an action plan after an inspection and monitoring how the plan is put into practice.

A. Holt (1993) reported guidelines from AGIT (Action for Governors' Information and Training) which stated that governors were there to:

- advise;
- provide a different perspective and alternative information;
- make policy and set priorities;
- mediate different views, initially amongst themselves;
- support and promote, but with careful thought about the kind of support required;
- monitor, bearing in mind the Secretary of State's intention to place accountability on the governing body and the head together.

Neither of these lists refers to the governors' responsibility for the school premises and for health and safety, yet these are important. The 1997 edition of *School Governors: A Guide to the Law* also includes a chart giving the responsibilities of headteachers and governors. This lists the following under health and safety:

- make sure buildings, equipment and materials are safe and no risk to health;
- set up procedures for implementing the H and S policy and make sure they are followed;
- keep land free from litter and refuse.

The following are listed under 'School Building':

- control use of premises outside school day;
- follow LEA directions on community use outside school hours;
- consider needs of local community;
- may enter into agreement allowing shared management of the premises.

Keys and Fernandez (1990) found that 42 per cent of governors, 60 per cent of governor headteachers and 70 per cent of non-governor headteachers thought the responsibilities of governors were too high. Fifty-four per cent of governors, 40 per cent of governor headteachers and 30 per cent of non-governor headteachers thought the responsibilities were about right and 5 per cent of governors, but no headteachers, thought the responsibilities too little.

By 1994, when Earley surveyed governors, the governors thinking the responsibilities were too great had dropped to about a third and the number of heads overall with this view had dropped to two-thirds. In both studies finance and budgetary matters were most often mentioned by governors as being heavy responsibilities along with appointments, personnel issues and the National Curriculum. Earley reports that headteachers, more than chairs or governors, more frequently made reference to the curriculum and decision making/policy making as areas where governors had too much responsibility.

In both studies governors felt that the most rewarding activities were involvement in decision making, developing relationships with other governors and relationships with the school in general.

Establishing aims and policies

Earley (1994) reports that in the case-study schools governors did not actually make policies but commented on policy making by the school and agreed policies once made. This suggests that it is important that governors are involved at an early stage when policies are being formed so that they have a genuine chance to contribute to the thinking behind the policy. If they are simply presented with the finished article they may do no more than spend time arguing over details of wording. In one governing body, for example, where the school was working out its curriculum policy, the members of the governors' curriculum and assessment committee worked in pairs to set down the things they would like to see in the policy. This gave the school a starting point and ensured that governors had thought about the content of the policy.

Governors also have a responsibility for monitoring the effect of policies, and this is not easy. In the case of the curriculum policy the committee concerned monitored by visiting and observing, by inviting teachers to come and talk about their work and by getting reports on the outcome of the SATs and other internal tests. They might also have used such things as the levels of reading at appropriate points in the school.

The responsibility as it is set out in the DfEE booklet (1997b) also requires governors to consider with the head how the standards of education can be improved. Schools are now asked to set targets for improvement and governors must be involved with the head and staff in this exercise.

Deciding in general terms the conduct of the school

This will be largely a matter of discussing the proposals of the head and staff about the way the school is organised, the teaching strategies being employed, any changes in staffing, the behaviour policy and its implications, arrangements for the involvement of parents, health and safety arrangements, issues concerned with the school premises and other general matters. There will also be situations where parents have queried some aspect of the school's work and governors will want to raise these or be prepared to comment on them if the problem has been raised with the head. These may include situations where there is a problem about a member of staff or a pupil, including occasions where it may be necessary to declare a member of staff redundant.

If governors are to do this, they need to know the school well and be familiar with the way teachers work. This means that they should make every effort to visit the school when it is in session and observe in classrooms. One school, for example, arranged that two members of the governing body would visit every term and report back to the full group on their findings. If this is to be useful, governors must first learn about the way in which primary schools operate, so that they do not come in expecting a secondary school approach to work. The head and staff need to see that their governors are fully informed and find ways to induct new governors into the school's methods and strategies. One way of involving governors is for each governor to adopt a year group or a particular class and get to know the teachers and the way they work by visiting them during working hours. An alternative, particularly in middle schools, is for governors to take an interest in a particular subject and to visit to see the way it is taught throughout the school.

The school development plan

Governors need to be involved with the school development plan at an early stage so that they can contribute to the draft before it reaches a stage when changes are difficult because priorities are set. If the governing body has spent time with the staff thinking out a vision for the school, this is the point when vision and planning should come together.

Governors should be involved in selecting items for audit as a preliminary to making the plan. They then need to consider items they would like to see in the plan before the headteacher gets down to serious work on it. This should be regarded as a kind of shopping list, leaving the headteacher and senior staff free to decide on their priorities for the plan, but governors also may have some items they want to see as priorities.

The school budget

Governors share with the head the responsibility for the school's financial arrangements. Most schools have a committee looking at finance and keeping track of spending, as well as helping the headteacher to decide how money should be spent.

Ideally there should be delegation of aspects of the budget to individual teachers, such as coordinators, or groups of teachers, such as year teams, each of whom should put forward their plans for the next year and the cost of these, together with the cost of maintaining existing activities. The task then becomes one of working out how far these plans can be reconciled and met within the budget.

Strain (1990) suggests that there are two ways of looking at the budget. The school can take the previous year's budget and see how it needs modifying to meet the coming year's expenditure. This is called incremental budgeting; it gives stability and is time-saving but may neglect problems. An alternative is zero budgeting which involves reconsidering spending each year. Most schools use a combination of these two ways of working.

Rolph (1990) lists the following categories of expenditure:

- salaries;
- energy costs;
- local taxation;
- equipment (education) purchases;
- resource materials – library, etc. (education);
- equipment (maintenance and administration);
- services (educational, maintenance, insurance);
- rental cost of equipment;
- staff training and travel.

It is the responsibility of the governors to see that the school has clear systems for authorising expenditure and controlling it. Most schools today will keep their accounts on computer and this makes it possible to produce printouts of how things are going on a regular basis. The governors' annual report to parents also needs to include a statement of the way money has been spent.

The teaching of the National Curriculum and religious education

The Ofsted report *Subjects and Standards* (1994/5 : 26) notes that there are schools where there is an unsatisfactory balance of subjects, with design and technology, religious education, history, geography and art under-represented: 'Imbalance is sometimes associated with an unproductive and inefficient use of time in mathematics and English.' The report states that at least a quarter of schools do not provide systematic teaching of religious education. Governors need to be familiar with the policy statements for these subjects and ask questions about how they are taught, as well as observing lessons.

The responsibility of governors for religious education also extends to seeing that there is a daily act of worship which is broadly Christian in nature. This is not easy in current circumstances because in many cases teachers are not prepared to support what would formerly have been considered the normal content of the act of worship, and schools have turned to assemblies which set out to encourage broad principles and values, which are usually Christian in character, and to reflect on the work of the school. All governing bodies should give careful consideration to whether the school is conforming to the law.

Selecting the head and deputy, and appointing, promoting, supporting and disciplining other staff

Governors will have varied experience of making appointments. Some will be familiar with the interviewing process in other employment and may simply need to become familiar with the slightly different practices in education. Others will have no experience of interviewing and appointing, and it is important that there is some in-service provision for the governing body so that all governors are in a position to make a contribution to appointments.

Staff need to feel that governors support their work. Occasions for teachers to talk to governors about the way they work provide opportunities for governors to express support and the relationships with staff that governors gradually develop can also create a feeling of support. In some schools individual governors are encouraged to link with a particular class and get to know the work of that class and teacher.

At the same time governors have responsibility for the discipline of staff. This may sometimes be a matter of dealing with failing teachers with a view to dismissal or it may be a less serious matter. Governors need to be very clear about their responsibilities in these situations and to take advice about the best way of moving forward. It should be remembered that the governors who deal with a case in the first instance must be different from those who deal with any appeal.

Acting as a link between the local community and the school

Governors, particularly parent governors, will often hear views about the school from parents and other members of the community. These enable them to keep the school informed about the way in which it is viewed locally. Governors who know the school well are also in a position to keep local people informed about aspects of the school's work which may perhaps be misinterpreted by those with less contact. It is therefore important that governors share the vision of the head and staff and can help to make it widely appreciated and understood.

Drawing up an action plan after an inspection and monitoring how the plan is put into practice

Inspection reports usually give very clear indications of what needs to be done and the process of making an action plan is usually shared between the governors and the headteacher and senior staff. The plan should have clear objectives that can be seen to be achieved, making monitoring its progress easier. Monitoring will include receiving reports from the headteacher about progress being made and also making observations.

Special educational needs

The law under the 1996 Education Act gives governors the following responsibilities for special educational needs:

- Make every effort to see that the necessary special arrangements are made for any pupil who has special educational needs.
- Make sure that the 'responsible person' makes all staff who are likely to teach the pupil aware of those needs. The 'responsible person' is generally the head, but may be the chairman of governors or a governor appointed by the governing body to take that responsibility. If the 'responsible person' is the head, it may be helpful for one other governor also to have an interest in special needs.
- Make sure that the teachers in the school are aware of the importance of identifying pupils who have special educational needs and of providing appropriate teaching.
- Consult the LEA and the governing bodies of other schools when it is necessary to coordinate special educational teaching in the area.
- Make arrangements for pupils with special educational needs to join in the everyday activities of the school as far as is practical.
- Report each year to parents on their policy for pupils with special educational needs.
- Take account of the Code of Practice when carrying out their duties towards all pupils with special educational needs.

(DfEE 1997b : 34)

The governors' role in monitoring the work of the school

Many of the tasks listed above involve governors in monitoring the work of the school. The following list of ways of monitoring is adapted from one drawn up by one governing body:

1 Information available about the school

- inspection reports;
- Standard Attainment Task results;
- attendance records;
- school development plan;
- curriculum plans;
- financial information;
- headteacher's reports to governors;
- newsletters to parents.

2 *Ways of seeking information*

- visits to the school;
- observation of teaching;
- questionnaires to parents, staff, children;
- discussion with parents, staff, children;
- governor links with particular classes;
- attendance at school events – assemblies, concerts, plays, etc.;
- inviting staff to meetings to discuss their work;
- attendance at parents' evenings.

3 *Informal sources of information*

- appearance of the school – displays, cleanliness, etc.;
- staff/children relationships;
- behaviour of children about the school;
- behaviour of children at the beginning and end of school and at lunch times;
- relationship with staff;
- relationship with support staff;
- involvement with the PTA (parent governors);
- comments from members of the community.

Breakdown of responsibilities between the head and the governing body

The headteacher and the governing body

- must make sure that the National Curriculum and its assessment procedures are carried out in full.

The governing body

- decide in primary schools whether the school should provide sex education and keep a written record;
- decide the approach to religious education;
- decide in controlled schools, the policy for collective worship, after consulting the head;
- must hear any appeal against a head's decision to lift or change the National Curriculum requirements for a child, and may override that decision;
- must hear formal complaints from parents and others about the school's curriculum, according to procedures set up by the LEA;
- may change the LEA's curriculum policy to match their aims for

the school, as long as this fits in with the National Curriculum; and

- must send the school's assessment results in full (if this is appropriate).

The head

- is responsible for day-to-day decisions about the management and curriculum of the school;
- may decide that the National Curriculum will not apply or apply differently to an individual pupil for a temporary period;
- decides, in county schools, the arrangements for collective worship, after consulting the governing body;
- must give the marking agency pupils' answers to the Key Stage 2 and 3 tests (if this is appropriate).

(DfEE 1997b : 30)

Health and safety and premises

Governors have responsibility under the Health and Safety at Work Act (1974) for seeing that people working in the school are not exposed to risks to their health and safety. They also have to take reasonable care that visitors to the school will be safe on the premises and they need to see that there are first-aid facilities for the children. They must see that the school adheres to the LEA's health and safety policy and that the school has its own policy for health and safety. They must review the building and equipment from time to time from the safety point of view.

The community

Schools are part of their local community, and although their major links are through governors and parents, they also have other links, some professional and some more general.

Links with other schools

Any school's major links are with its contributory and transfer schools. Schools with infants on roll also need to link with playgroups and nursery schools contributing children to them.

Continuity is essential for children as they move through the school system and it is in the hands of the schools concerned to see that the transfers are as smooth as possible. It is worth making time to talk with children transferring about their fears and hopes for their new school. One study of transfer from primary to secondary school found the majority of children worrying about bullying, homework and getting lost, though these proved to be largely unfounded worries (Dean 1997). They also worried about strict teachers, whether the work would be too hard, and older pupils. The more that can be done to ease these worries, the better, and this is more likely if there is a good relationship between the schools concerned. It is not usually possible for junior, middle or secondary schools to work with all the schools which may be contributing children to them but there are usually major contributory schools and visits can be arranged for both teachers and children.

It is also possible to avoid overmuch repetition of curriculum if there is good communication, although it must be recognised that some repetition is inevitable as there is a case for revision to ensure that everyone has covered the ground. It helps if there are opportunities for teachers in the receiving school to discuss with teachers in the sending school the work which they normally expect to cover. The National Curriculum is some help, as are the SATs results, but this information is usually too broad to build on. The lifting of the requirements for schools to follow the different subjects of the National Curriculum in detail, except in the cases of English, mathematics and science, makes continuity less assured and further necessitates that schools work together.

There is much to be said for sending a small representative sample of work with each child. However, this is of no use if teachers do not look at it, and at the secondary stage in particular teachers deal with many children and are unlikely to spend much time studying information about individuals. Teachers are also inclined to say that they want to make up their own minds about individual children rather than being influenced by someone else's opinion. Records should not be opinions but factual information about what a child is able to do and has done. It is possible at primary/secondary transfer for sending schools to provide a statement of the work covered by each class as a whole under subject headings. This is more likely to be read and can be more easily taken into account than individual records.

It is particularly important to study transfer information about children with special needs and any who are exceptionally able. Children who know that they are not very able compared with some classmates are often worried about showing their problems in a new school and it is helpful if teachers there are aware of what they can and cannot do, and can move on from the stage reached in the previous school. Special needs departments in secondary schools should encourage their colleagues to find out about children with special needs. The very able can also be held back if teachers are not aware of their ability. These issues also apply when children move from first or infant school to junior or middle school.

Parents need reassurance at stages of transfer and they will want to know details of school routines and ways of keeping in touch. They should be encouraged to talk to teachers about their children, particularly where children have problems such as asthma or a history of absence through illness, or home problems like a handicapped sibling.

There is also a case for making links with other schools working with the same age groups, particularly where the school is small. In some authorities there is encouragement and provision for small schools to collaborate, perhaps sharing specialist staff or arranging joint trips or activities for particular groups of children. Small schools have difficulty in providing specialist support across the curriculum and by collaborating schools can have the benefit of a greater range of expertise. Some joint training days for staff may be a possibility. Bentley (1991) describes a project in North Yorkshire where money was allocated to a group of small schools for collaborative work, including the appointment of a project coordinator, an advisory teacher and a secretary who also drove a jointly owned minibus available for any of the schools to use. This resulted in considerable staff development and opportunities for children to work with larger peer groups. Other authorities have run similar schemes.

The locality as a learning resource

The school is part of the local community and the community and the environment provide valuable first-hand material for the children's learning in many aspects of the curriculum. The local environment provides opportunities for mathematical, scientific, historical and geographical study as well as opportunities to develop artwork, drama, dance, music and both reflective and factual writing. Links with local industry may be valuable in helping children to understand how industry works. The local environment also offers opportunities to study local and national government and their effect on the community.

Learning needs to be applied if it is to be useful and it is in the context of the local environment and community that children can use what they are learning. Children also need to be encouraged to feel responsible for their local environment.

There will also be people in the community as well as parents who have skills and knowledge that they may be prepared to share with children. Local services are often ready to demonstrate some of the things they do. Local craftspeople may be prepared to show their work and to suggest ways in which the children can explore similar activities. Teachers need to know their community and environment well so that they can exploit the opportunities it offers for children's learning.

12

EVALUATION

A small study of the use of time by primary headteachers (Dean 1995a) found that no time at all was allowed for formal evaluation of the work of the school. When this was discussed all the headteachers protested that they were evaluating all the time but did this informally in the process of moving about the school, talking with teachers and children, observing what was happening, and so on.

This finding was confirmed by the Ofsted report, *Primary Matters* (1994b : 28), which found that 'Few schools had effective and comprehensive monitoring and evaluation systems.' The report went on to describe what was happening as follows:

> In just over a quarter of the schools (27 per cent) a range of strategies was employed. For example, the headteachers and/or senior management team regularly scrutinised teachers' plans; made visits to classrooms; taught across a range of classes, often to provide non-contact time for those with subject responsibility; attended group planning meetings and arranged times to review curriculum coverage and systems for planning. However, in only two of these schools did headteachers attempt systematically to monitor the standards of work achieved by pupils. In one school the headteacher interviewed six pupils from two different year groups each week and went through their work with them. In the other school the headteacher and senior management team regularly scrutinised together samples of pupils' work in the core subjects.

Bradley (1988 : 2) makes the following points about evaluation:

> Where evaluation is seen as essential and non-threatening, where there is always an expectation that things can be improved, where there is an expectation that mistakes will be made and that such events are normal, then individuals blossom.

Purposes of evaluation

Stoll and Fink (1996 : 168–9) make the following statements about the purposes of evaluation:

> We believe that the key purposes for any judgements of school quality should be to:
>
> - Promote school self-accountability, translatable into wider accountability – teachers and principals need to know how they make a difference to their pupils' progress, development and attainment.
> - Provide useful indicators of what works well and what needs to be improved – it is important to know what works well so that it can be celebrated and analysed to understand its success.
> - Guarantee equal opportunities for all pupils.
> - Determine trends in school effectiveness and improvement over time – teachers need to know if their school is improving or declining over a period of years.
> - Lead to further development – information on school's effectiveness and improvement is only helpful if it is used.

A different analysis suggests that evaluation serves four different purposes in a school. As we have seen, it is needed for accountability. Schools need to demonstrate that they are working successfully. Evaluation is also essential for management. The way in which money is spent should be considered: is the school getting value for money? Headteachers have to decide which teachers take which classes, and this means being aware of the characteristics of both teachers and children. There are decisions to be made about developments which require background information. In fact most aspects of management depend upon effective evaluation of what is happening in the school.

Evaluation is important in deciding in the classroom what to do next and what particular help an individual child may need. There is much evidence to suggest that teachers must reflect on their work and evaluate what they do. The importance of using evaluation and assessment to give feedback to children about their progress and adapt teaching to the findings of the evaluation was stressed in Chapter 7.

Finally, evaluation is needed for accreditation. This is more relevant in the secondary than the primary school, but the assessment at the end of the Key Stages forms a kind of accreditation for the children concerned. The Key Stage 1 assessment may set teachers' expectations for the child as he or she enters the junior school or department. The same applies for the tests at the end of Key Stage 2 which will affect the child moving into the secondary school.

Evaluation and planning

Evaluation is too important to leave entirely to informal activity. While this is undoubtedly valuable, it is unsystematic and may leave important areas of the life and work of the school unconsidered. The school needs both an evaluation and assessment policy, and an evaluation plan which over time covers all aspects of its life and work. However, it is easy to attempt too much evaluation at one time and the activity should be spread so that each year some particular aspects are evaluated in a formal and systematic way as well as formal and informal evaluation of the main business of the school – children's learning.

Ofsted (1994a : 21) describes the relationship of planning and evaluation as follows:

> Evaluation lets the school see whether its planning has been successful, how far it has achieved what it set out to achieve. The school uses a number of performance indicators to measure how well it is doing. Teachers' routine planning of the work indicates what is intended to be achieved in respect of individuals, classes and year groups, and so provides a set of base-lines against which success can be measured. In management terms, planning enables clear and sharp monitoring of all members of staff.

Rogers and Badham (1994 : 103) suggest that the planned evaluation is characterised by:

- agreed target areas for evaluation;
- explicitness about criteria for the evaluation of success;
- an evaluation plan which outlines who will collect the data, when, and what will be the source of the information;
- a systematic approach to the collection and recording of information where all involved use appropriate, agreed evaluation instruments.

There are three levels at which evaluation needs to be carried out. At the school level headteachers and governors need a profile of the school in relation to other similar schools, and many LEAs are providing this kind of information. A range of examples is given in Tabberer (1997). They need to know if the school is adding value, given the intake. This involves information about such data as the numbers with free school meals, the numbers with special needs and with Statements; the baseline for children entering the school. This then needs to be matched with information about what the children are achieving and it is helpful to know what other schools are achieving with similar intakes.

Headteachers and governors should know costs in relation to the number of pupils. These may be the costs of teachers, ancillaries and administrative staff, caretaking, supplies and services, and so on. Here again it is helpful to know comparable figures for similar schools.

A school should also make comparisons between one year and another. Are results in terms of tests improving? Different years vary in overall ability so that one year may do less well without any reflection on the quality of teaching, but if results are monitored over a number of years patterns can emerge. Attendance may be monitored from year to year, as can costs of different parts of the school's work.

Evaluation is also necessary at the classroom level. Headteachers need to know the abilities of their teachers, and this can only be judged by observation, discussion and information about children's progress. This information forms a basis for considering staff development which should be evaluated in terms of the effect it has on performance in the classroom as well as how helpful teachers consider it to be. Teachers in the classroom must constantly evaluate their work and schools should encourage teachers to be reflective.

The third area in which evaluation needs to take place is in relation to the children. Teachers should assess and record individual progress, as well as making judgments about the progress of the whole class. Shipman (1990 : 119) notes that assessment 'is central to matching the curriculum to the attainment of children, to sequencing work and giving it the right place'. Pupils can be compared with each other or against predetermined criteria. Stoll and Fink (1996 : 125) suggest that teachers need 'to determine standards of performance at the beginning of the teaching/learning process rather than at the end'. Children also need to be encouraged to evaluate their own work in all aspects of the curriculum.

Askew *et al.* (1997) studied highly effective teachers of numeracy. One of their findings was that teachers who were highly effective used assessment to inform their teaching, whereas teachers who were less effective used it more to judge whether what had been taught had been learned.

Gipps *et al.* (1995) studied the effect on teachers of the requirement to assess children as part of the testing at Key Stages 1 and 2. They found that:

> In 1991 many of our Year 2 teachers, in preparation for teacher assessment, began to do three things:
>
> * collect evidence of children's work which they would then save as proof, including such things as photographs (especially in science) and tape recordings of reading;
> * use observation (especially in mathematics and science) as a technique of assessment;
> * record the information.
>
> In particular some teachers took detailed notes of their observations, questioned children closely to determine understanding, and planned assessment into their teaching.
>
> (Gipps *et al.* 1995 : 23)

Overall the authors found that for many teachers the requirements of teacher assessment had made a difference to the way they assessed. One teacher commented, 'A lot of assessment used to be a gut feeling but now I am going back and checking. I'm observing children far more thoroughly and doing more talking to them' (p.26).

Mortimore *et al.* (1988 : 223) found that:

> Pupil progress and development tended to be promoted in those schools where the headteacher requested the staff to keep individual records of children's work and where those records were discussed by the head and the class teachers concerned. In addition the practice of class teachers passing on folders of children's work to their next teacher was also related to positive effects on progress.

This suggests that teachers who take the view that they want to start with a 'clean slate' may be misguided.

Teachers should also assess group work. This means not only assessing what has been achieved by the children in a group, but whether they are fulfilling the aims of group work. Are they learning to listen to each other, ask good questions, work cooperatively, support each other, and so on?

Schools must also be concerned with children's records of achievement which should record not only progress in school but out-of-school activities that may be informative about the individual child.

Performance indicators should be identified. Preedy *et al.* (1997 : 33) suggest that performance indicators should:

- be about the school's performance;
- be central to the process of teaching and learning;
- cover significant parts of the school's activities (but not all);
- reflect competing educational priorities;
- be capable of being assessed;
- allow meaningful comparisons over time and between schools;
- allow schools to be seen to have changed their levels of performance by dint of their own efforts;
- be few in number.

The school development plan

Evaluation needs to be part of the school development plan from the beginning. A review of what has been recently evaluated is the starting point for the plan and all the items in the plan need to involve evaluation. As the plan is being worked out evaluation should be considered since considering how to evaluate an item is helpful in setting targets or performance indicators which are sufficiently clearly defined to tell if they have been achieved. MacGilchrist *et al.* (1995), studying school development plans, found that the most noticeable weakness was in relation to monitoring and evaluating.

Evaluation of the school development plan must be reported to governors at regular intervals, and the evaluation will, in turn, be reflected in the next year's plan. There is also a need to report to staff from time to time on how the plan is going. The staff might ask themselves whether they achieved what they set out to achieve, whether the school has changed as a result of a particular development, and whether the change is what they intended?

In addition to considering whether the targets identified in the plan are being achieved there is a case for evaluating the plan itself. Skelton *et al.* (1991 : 119) suggest the following questions:

- Do staff feel they own the plan?
- Have we got the right time scales?
- Have we defined responsibilities?
- Is there something for everyone in the plan?
- Has anyone got too much to do?
- Has everyone got access to adequate professional support?
- Are the targets clearly stated?
- Will we know if we have been successful?
- How did we set about achieving this target?
- Why did we not achieve this target?
- Do we have the support of the governors?
- Do we have the support of the parents?
- What effect are we having on the children's learning?

The role of governors

Governors have an overall responsibility for their schools and most governing bodies are exercised in their minds about how this responsibility can best be discharged. How does a group of laypeople make sensible judgments about how well a school is doing? They will, of course, be informed by Ofsted inspections, but the gap between inspections is a long one. They will also have information about how the school is doing in the tests at Key Stages, but if they are to interpret these results, they need to know how the school compares with other schools with similar intake.

What other things can governors do? They will receive regular reports from their headteacher but these will tend to be reports from a particular point of view. They will also hear the views of parents, which will give them an idea of how happy parents are with what the school is doing. We have already noted that an important activity for governors is that of visiting the school while it is in session and spending time in classrooms, not in the role of inspectors but in order to get to know how the school is working. It is helpful if governors

compare notes about what they have seen, since this will help them to understand what is going on.

Another possibility is for individual teachers to meet governors, either as a
complete group or in committees to report on how they go about their work.
This might be in general terms or might be part of helping governors to
understand how particular parts of the curriculum are undertaken. A series of
meetings, for example, might be about how reading or number is taught or
how a particular project has worked out.

Governors could undertake questionnaire surveys of parents or older children. Questions can be asked about how well parents feel the school
communicates with them, whether they feel their children are making the
progress they should and whether there are areas in which they would like
more information. Children at the top end of the primary school can be asked
about what they enjoy or dislike, whether they feel they are making progress
and whether they would recommend the school to parents moving into the
area. This kind of activity must be undertaken in cooperation with the school
but it offers the headteacher and staff, as well as the governors, valuable
information.

Planning evaluation

We have already noted that evaluation needs to be part of the planning of all
aspects of the life and work of the school. It should also be carefully planned.
In some instances it requires targets which can be seen to be achieved and the
defining of success criteria. In other situations, such as in evaluating the work
in personal and social education, there may or may not be targets but there
must be success criteria.

Evaluation needs to take account of the starting point for any activity. There
is current consideration of baseline assessments of children entering school, and
children entering a junior school or department will come with the Key Stage
1 assessment that gives a base from which to measure progress. There is some
doubt, however, about the validity and reliability of testing at school entry.
Clark (1989 : 35) makes the following comment about some of her research,
which involved testing pre-school children: 'We were able to show from the
materials we had from different tests administered to the same child how
much a young child might be influenced by the form of the question and
whether or not further probing was permitted to encourage a more extended
response.' However, the sort of baseline testing which is being considered
will allow some probing and will give teachers some useful information to
guide early work.

Scheerens (1992 : 102) suggests that:

> School evaluation at the various levels of school organisation requires
> certain skills: knowledge about data collection methods, techniques to

retrieve, store, process and analyse data, possibly using computers for these functions, and skills of reporting and feeding back evaluation results.

Evidence for evaluation

In planning evaluation consideration should be given to what will be used as evidence. There will be documentary evidence which gives the starting points, such as information about the school compared with other similar schools, policies, schemes of work, the school development plan, teachers' plans, and so on. There will be quantitative evidence, such as attendance records, financial records, teachers' records of the progress of individual children and test results. There will also be qualitative evidence, such as observation of changes in practice like extended team planning and more interactive whole-class teaching; teachers' plans may show what was intended and this can be considered alongside what happened. Teachers' records may also include notes about individual children and how they are progressing.

A very important collection of evidence is in the children's work and what they have to say about it. Does this show evidence of progress? Is their understanding increasing? What have they achieved? How widespread is achievement? How many children appear to be standing still or even slipping back? This needs assessing at the classroom level but headteachers should also be evaluating what is happening in classrooms, sampling children's skills and work on a regular basis and talking with them about what they understand and how they feel things are going.

There will be evidence from discussion, perhaps reflecting changes in attitude about work on the part of both teachers and children. A school may survey parental opinion or the views of older children. Some of this evidence will be gathered informally and some may be the subject of more formal evaluation.

Evaluation will be easier if targets are used, both at the class level and at the individual level. The National Numeracy Project *Draft Framework for Numeracy* (1997) suggests that teachers should have a ten-minute conference with each child once a term. This involves setting targets for him or her and communicating these to parents, involving them if possible in supporting the child in achieving the targets. Progress is then monitored.

Ofsted (1994a : 39) suggests that as a way of evaluating topic work there should be a review written by the teacher at the end of the topic. This should be a 'personal evaluation of the success of the topic. The head meets each teacher individually, goes through the report and, after discussion, new targets for the next half-term are set.'

Preedy *et al.* (1997 : 66) suggest that it is useful to have data on the following:

- The levels achieved in specific subjects by girls and boys as they progress through school;
- The progress made by children from different social class or ethnic group;
- The impact of teaching styles, curriculum innovation, ways of involving parents, managing the school;
- The resources allocated to SEN and their attainment.

Personnel, time and costs

Another important part of planning evaluation is deciding who will undertake particular evaluation tasks. These should be spread so that no one is overburdened. The time such tasks will take has to be considered and this may lead to some costs in that a teacher may need to be freed from a class in order to undertake some aspect of evaluation. A school anticipating an Ofsted inspection may also wish to buy in a survey by local advisers in order to prepare for the inspection.

Helping children to evaluate their work

If children are to become independent learners they need to become competent at evaluating their own work. The teacher can do a good deal to encourage this. It may start with children evaluating each other's work. In a subject like art, this is very easy. A group of children can look at the work they have done and discuss it. The teacher can encourage a positive approach by asking them to say what they like about individual pieces of work and what they think would improve them. Topic work can also be treated in this way. Similar work can be done about written work in pairs, with children reading what others have written, checking for errors and commenting on what seems to be good in the work.

Teachers can also encourage self-evaluation by the questions they ask when looking at a piece of work. They can ask what the child thinks about the work and whether there are ways in which he or she could make it better. If targets have been set, they can ask the child to evaluate it against the targets if this is appropriate. The comments which teachers write on children's work can also encourage self-evaluation.

Needham (1994 : 159) suggests using evaluation sheets in which children complete unfinished sentences such as, 'Something I'm good at is . . .', 'Something I'd like to be good at is . . .'. She also suggests getting children to write about how they feel about a piece of work they have finished. This might be particularly appropriate with topic work, where a group might compile a report on the work they have done. Discussion about work is an important way of making children critical and self-critical.

Muschamp (1994 : 235) suggests giving children guidance in assessing their work. The teacher might ask 'Did you . . .?' questions. The child might then be asked how the work might be improved with questions such as, 'Can I think of another way I could have done this?', 'Could I have made this activity easier?', 'How could I have made this better?'

Alexander (1984 : 213) makes the following comment about evaluation, which to some extent puts it in context:

> Teachers' and heads' use of tests, checklist, profiles and so on constitutes a minute proportion of the evaluation on which their most important everyday decisions are made. The *focus* is on children's personalities, their potential, their behaviour, their educational progress. The *aims* are diagnosis, making necessarily rapid decisions as a basis for further action. The *criteria* are personal, experiential, value-loaded, sometimes idiosyncratic, sometimes collectively involved. The *methods* are watching, talking, listening, giving out and receiving non-verbal cues and signals, reflecting, hypothesising, discussing.

13

CONCLUSION

The Government White Paper *Excellence in Schools* (DfEE 1997a : 43) makes the following points about the future of education:

> Across many sectors of the economy and many aspects of our lives, the pace of innovation is dramatic. New thinking about leadership and management, operational research, new uses of ICT and the ever-increasing pressure for high quality have led to a transformation in many knowledge-based industries. Teaching and learning should not be exempt from this revolution.
>
> It is striking that so far the teaching and learning process has stayed remarkably stable in spite of the huge structural changes of the last decade or so. We believe that, as the pressure of international competition increases and we face up to the demands of the twenty-first century, we must expect change in the nature of schooling.

Preedy *et al.* (1997 : 2) identify the external pressures on education at present as follows:

1　Educational issues – concerns about the performance of schools and colleges expressed by governments, the inspectorate and the public at large;
2　Political issues – concerns about reducing public spending as a proportion of the GDP and the demands of education vis-à-vis other public expenditure priorities;
3　Economic arguments – concerns about the links between educational spending and economic success, especially in comparison with competitor nations.

Schools have been subjected to a barrage of criticism and advice on how to do better over recent years. The excellent work done by some primary schools working along Plowden (Central Advisory Council for Education 1967) lines has been largely ignored and there has been a concentration on those schools which have done badly. There was much that was good going on during the so-called trendy sixties and seventies and teachers need to cling on to what they know to be successful while at the same time reflecting on their work and looking at what research is being shown to be effective.

Budge (1997 : 17) reports Professor Robin Alexander speaking at a seminar at Warwick University as making the following points about comparing British education with that of other countries:

- It is a mistake to try to raise literacy and numeracy standards by downgrading the rest of the curriculum. Equally reading and writing should not be emphasised at the expense of talk. (HMI made a similar point in their study of primary schools in 1978 where they found that a narrow concentration on basic skills was less successful than a broad curriculum.)
- Whole-class teaching is not a guarantor of educational success. It is also associated with failure worldwide.
- Teacher-initiated question and answers is not the only effective form of classroom interaction.
- The importance of time on task has been over-stressed. The pace and structure of lessons are actually more significant.
- There is no direct and causal link between pedagogy, attainment in literacy and national economic competitiveness.

We are at a stage of rapid change in almost every aspect of our lives. We should think a great deal about what we want our schools to achieve in the next century and the best way of achieving it. We shall shortly be looking at changes in the National Curriculum and we can hope that these will be changes which are not too demanding for teachers, who need space to do their own thinking and reflection.

What is needed in education at the primary stage in the future? The possibilities of information technology could change the face of teaching very considerably. So far we have seen the computer mainly as an aid to work with the teacher. The Internet offers an enormous resource for this work and schools must learn to use it profitably. What has been little explored so far is the computer as a teaching tool in its own right. There are many areas where good programs might actually take on the role of the teacher, assess the stage the individual child has reached and provide for the next stage of learning.

The classroom of the future might be individualised in a new way for some work. This leads to a consideration of what it is important to do in a group, whether a whole-class group, a small group or even a pair. Discussion is important for learning in all subjects and some, such as drama, aspects of physical education and music, require groups for their successful teaching.

Information technology also provides opportunities for links with other countries through the Internet and e-mail, and this can help to develop a

European and a whole-world view for children. It seems likely that there will be increasing pressure to teach other languages at the primary stage. At present there is a shortage of modern language teachers at all levels and this must change. People in other countries are often much more fluent in English than British children are in other languages, and many countries teach a second language at the primary stage.

Another area where we are likely to see development is in the education of the exceptionally able. We have seen a good deal of concern about the less able and children with special educational needs and we must recognise that very able children also have special needs which we are not doing enough to meet at the present time.

The government is showing concern about the education of very young children, an area in which we are less well provided than many other countries, but consideration must also be given to education for parenthood. This is something which some secondary schools used to offer but now no longer have time for, with the pressures of the National Curriculum. We know that parents are enormously influential for their children, particularly in the early years, and one way of raising the ability of all children would be to ensure that all prospective parents knew something about children's early learning and development. Many primary schools are doing their best to involve parents in children's learning with schemes such as paired reading and, less commonly, mathematics work. Nursery schools and playgroups are also helping to educate parents into ways of preparing their children for school. These schemes must be adopted more widely.

The National Curriculum does not put forward any aims for the education service although they might be said to be implicit in the programmes of study. Schools must be clear about their aims, and these need to be wide ranging. Forward (1988 : 61–2) suggests the following aims for primary education:

1 To help pupils become knowledgeable and skilful in relevant and enriching ways.
2 To give the pupils information gathering skills, including literacy and numeracy, which will enable them to inform themselves as the need arises.
3 To give pupils the skills needed to order, validate, evaluate and interpret information and also to begin to internalise concepts which are vital to good judgement, particularly those that relate to the kind of adult society they are likely to live in.
4 To give pupils opportunities for using information to make rational choices, decisions and judgements. From these activities to foster the ability to think independently and critically while deepening self-knowledge and understanding their own emotions and needs.
5 To teach children the importance of encompassing all judgements

with consideration for others and to actively promote qualities of tolerance, compassion and kindness.

In considering aims we might also look at what we mean when we talk of an educated person and what contribution the primary school makes to this. In the first place educated people have achieved sufficient maturity and balance as individuals to cope with major change, as well as the stresses and conflicts of daily living. They will have developed their own framework of meaning and values for life which informs and governs their behaviour and enables them to choose and act with wisdom. They will have a self-image which is realistic but confident, based on good knowledge of their own strengths and limitations, and they will be independent in many aspects of living.

They will enjoy learning and will have developed in their initial education a sufficient knowledge of the underlying ideas in the major areas of human knowledge to enable them to continue learning. Alongside this, they will have developed more general skills of study. They will be able to think things through and will be good at solving problems, whether these are practical problems or more academic ones. They will be good at learning from observation at first hand and by questioning other people, as well as good at learning from books. They will be able to sort out ideas and information so that they can use it to tackle problems and meet demands made upon them. They will also have ideas, will know how to use them and be receptive to ideas coming from others.

They will have developed the skills of communication to a high level in a number of modes, so that they are not only able to speak and write fluently and appropriately, but are skilled at communicating graphically, mathematically and through movement. They will enjoy and practise the arts and take pleasure in fine craftsmanship. They will enjoy and care for the environment and feel responsibility towards it.

They will have learned to live with others, will be sensitive to them, skilled in understanding and responsible and caring in their attitudes. They will have the ability to cooperate in various roles within a group and will have learned democratic modes of behaviour. They will have knowledge of how individuals and societies function and will have been prepared for adult life as a citizen, a worker, a parent and a family member.

All of these abilities and skills will be of limited value if education has not succeeded in helping the individual to achieve happiness and enjoyment in life. Many of the aims above are contained in this. It is doubtful if people are happy unless they get on well with others. Happiness means achieving some kind of balance as an individual with developed skills and an ability to cope with the choices and conflicts which are part of the human condition.

Everything that happens to children, in and out of school, contributes to their development and learning. Everyone has a responsibility for the development of the young.

REFERENCES

Alexander, R. (1984) *Primary Teaching*, London: Holt, Rinehart and Winston

Alexander, R. (1992) *Policy and Practice in the Primary School*, London: Routledge

Alexander, R., Rose, J. and Woodhead, C. (1992) *Curriculum Organisation and Classroom Practice in Primary Schools*, London: Department of Education and Science

Alexander, R., Willcocks, J. and Kinder, K. (1989) *Changing Primary Practice*, London: Falmer Press

Askew, M. and Williams, D. (1995) *Recent Research in Mathematics Education*, London: HMSO for Ofsted

Askew, M., Brown, M., Rhodes, V., Johnson, D. and William, D. (1997) *Effective Teachers of Numeracy*, King's College, London, for the Teacher Training Agency

Aspinall, K., Simkins, T., Wilkinson, J.F. and McAuley, M.J. (1997) 'Using success criteria', in Preedy, M., Glatter, R. and Levacic, R. (eds) *Educational Management: Strategy, Quality and Resources*, Buckingham: Open University Press

Atkin, J., Bastiani, J. and Good, J. (1988) *Listening to Parents*, London: Croom Helm

Ayles, R. (1996) 'Differentiation? Working with more able children', in Croll, P. and Hastings, N. (eds) *Effective Primary Teaching: Research-based Classroom Strategies*, London: David Fulton Publishing

Bagley, C., Woods, P. and Glatter, R. (1997) 'Scanning the market: school strategies for discovering parental preferences', in Preedy, M., Glatter, R. and Levacic, R. (eds) *Educational Management: Strategy, Quality and Resources*, Buckingham: Open University Press

Barnes, C. (1993) *Practical Marketing for Schools*, Oxford: Blackwell

Bassey, M. (1978) *Nine Hundred Primary School Teachers*, Windsor: National Foundation for Educational Research Publishing Company

Bastiani, J. (1993) 'Parents as partners: genuine progress or empty rhetoric?', in Munn, P. (ed.) *Parents and Schools: Customers, Managers or Partners*, London: Routledge

Beare, H., Caldwell, B. and Millikan, R.H. (1989) *Creating an Excellent School*, London: Routledge

Bennett, Neville (1976) *Teaching Styles and Pupils' Progress*, London: Open Books

Bennett, Neville and Dunne, E. (1992) *Managing Classroom Groups*, Hemel Hempstead: Simon and Schuster Education

Bennett, Neville and Kell, J. (1989) *A Good Start: Four-year-olds in Infant Schools*, London: Open Books

Bennett, Neville, Andrae, J., Hegarty, P. and Wade, B. (1980) *Open Plan Schools*, Slough: National Foundation for Educational Research for the Schools Council

Bennett, Neville, Deforges, C., Cockburn, A. and Wilkinson, B. (1984) *The Quality of Pupil Learning Experiences*, London: Lawrence Erlbaum Associates

Bennett, Neville, Wragg, E.C., Carre, C.G. and Carter, D.S.G. (1992) 'A longitudinal study of primary teachers' perceived competence in and concerns about National Curriculum implementation', *Research Papers in Education* 7(1): 53–78

Bennett, Nigel, Glatter, R. and Levacic, R. (eds) (1994) *Improving Educational Management through Research and Consultancy*, London: Paul Chapman Publishing

Bennis, W. and Nanus, B. (1985) *Leaders*, New York: Harper and Row

Bentley, M. (1991) 'Amplifying the educational opportunities in small rural schools', in Sullivan, M. (ed.) *Supporting Change and Development in the Primary School*, Harlow: Longman

Besag, V.E. (1989) *Bullies and Victims in Schools*, Buckingham: Open University Press

Biott, C. and Nias, J. (eds) (1992) *Working and Learning Together for Change*, Buckingham: Open University Press

Blatchford, P. (1989) *Playtime in the Primary School: Problems and Improvements*, Windsor: NFER–Nelson

Bourne, J. (ed.) (1994) *Thinking through Primary Practice*, London: Routledge, in association with the Open University

Boydell, D. (1978) *The Primary Teacher in Action*, London: Open Books

Braddy, S. (1988) 'Personal and social education in the infants school: a practical approach', in Lang, P. (ed.) *Thinking about Personal and Social Education in the Primary School*, Oxford: Blackwell

Bradley, H. (1988) 'Staff development and INSET', in Clarkson, M. (ed.) *Emerging Issues in Primary Education*, London: The Falmer Press

Bradley, H., Conner, C. and Southworth, G. (eds) (1994) *Developing Teachers, Developing Schools*, London: David Fulton Publishers, in association with the University of Cambridge Institute of Education

Budge, D. (1997) 'In search of foreign correspondences', *Times Educational Supplement*, 5 December: 17

Burns, J.M. (1978) *Leadership*, New York: Harper and Row

Calderhead, J. (1994) 'Teaching as a professional activity', in Pollard, A. and Bourne, J. (eds) *Teaching and Learning in the Primary School*, London: Routledge

Campbell, R.J. (1988) 'The "collegial" primary school', in Clarkson, M. (ed.) *Emerging Issues in Primary Education*, London: The Falmer Press

Campbell, R.J. (1991) 'Curriculum coordinators and the National Curriculum', in Sullivan, M. (ed.) *Supporting Change and Development in the Primary School*, Harlow: Longman

Campbell, R.J. and Neill, S.R.StJ. (1994) *Primary Teachers at Work*, London: Routledge

Canter, L. (1979) 'Competency based approach to discipline – it's assertive', *Thrust for Educational Leadership*, 11–13 January

Cave, E. and Wilkinson, C. (eds) (1990) *Local Management of Schools: Some Practical Issues*, London: Routledge

Central Advisory Council for Education (England) (1967) *Children and Their Primary Schools* (The Plowden Report), London: HMSO

Charlton, T. (1988) 'Using counselling skills to enhance children's personal, social and academic functioning', in Lang, P. (ed.) *Thinking about Personal and Social Education in the Primary School*, Oxford: Blackwell

Clark, M.M. (1989) *Understanding Research in Early Education*, London: Gordon and Breach, Science Publishers

Clarkson, M. (ed.) (1988) *Emerging Issues in Primary Education*, London: The Falmer Press

Claxton, G. (1990) *Teaching to Learn: A Direction for Education*, London: Cassell

Clegg, D. and Billington, S. (1997) *Leading Primary Schools: The Pleasure, Pain and Principles of Being a Primary Headteacher*, Buckingham: Open University Press

Coleman, J., Campbell, E., Hobson, C., McPartland, J., Mood, A., Weinfeld, F. and York, R. (1966) *Equality of Educational Opportunity*, Washington, DC: United States Government Printing Office

Coles, M. (1997) 'Curriculum evaluation as review and development: the curriculum leader's role in creating a community of enquiry', in Preedy, M., Glatter, R. and Levacic, R. (eds) *Educational Management: Strategy, Quality and Resources*, Buckingham: Open University Press

Convey, A. (1992) 'Insight, direction and support: a case study of collaborative enquiry in classroom research', in Biott, C. and Nias, J. (eds) *Working and Learning Together for Change*, Buckingham: Open University Press

Cooper, P. and McIntyre, D. (1996) *Effective Learning and Teaching: Teachers' and Students' Perspectives*, Buckingham: Open University Press

Coulson, A.A. (1986) *The Management Work of the Primary School Headteacher*, Sheffield: Sheffield Papers in Education Management No. 48, Sheffield City Polytechnic

Creemers, B. (1994) 'The history, value and purpose of school effectiveness studies', in Reynolds, D., Creemers, B.P.M., Nesselrodt, P.S., Schaffer, E.C., Stringfield, S. and Teddlie, C. (eds) *Advances in School Effectiveness Research and Practice*, Oxford: Pergamon Press

Croll, P. and Hastings, N. (eds) (1996) *Effective Primary Teaching: Research-based Classroom Strategies*, London: David Fulton Publishing

Croll, P. and Moses, D. (1985) *One in Five: The Assessment and Incidence of Special Educational Needs*, London: Routledge and Kegan Paul

Cross, P. and Moses, N. (1988) 'Teaching methods and time on task in junior classrooms', *Educational Research* 30(2): 90–7

Cuttance, P. (1985) 'Framework for research on the effectiveness of schooling', in Reynolds, D. (ed.) *Studying School Effectiveness*, London: The Falmer Press

Cuttance, P. (1997) 'Monitoring educational quality', in Preedy, M., Glatter, R. and Levacic, R. (eds) *Educational Management: Strategy, Quality and Resources*, Buckingham: Open University Press

Day, C. and Moore, R. (eds) (1986) *Staff Development in the Secondary School*, London: Croom Helm

Day, C., Whitaker, P. and Wren, D. (1987) *Appraisal and Professional Development in Primary Schools*, Buckingham: Open University Press

Dean, J. (1991) *Professional Development in School*, Buckingham: Open University Press

Dean, J. (1995a) *The Use of Time by Primary School Headteachers*, Slough: Education Management Information Exchange, NFER

Dean, J. (1995b) *Managing the Primary School* (2nd edn), London: Routledge

Dean, J. (1997) 'Year 7 survey, St Crispin's School, Wokingham', unpublished report

Delamont, S. (ed.) (1987) *The Primary School Teacher*, London: The Falmer Press

Department for Education (1990) *Letter from Secretary of State to Chief Education Officers*, London: DfE

Department for Education and Employment (1994) *Code of Practice on the Identification and Assessment of Special Educational Needs*, London: Central Office of Information

Department for Education and Employment (1996) *Setting Targets to Raise Standards: A Survey of Good Practice*, London: Ofsted/DfEE

Department for Education and Employment (1997a) *Excellence in Schools*, London: DfEE

Department for Education and Employment (1997b) *School Governors: A Guide to the Law*, London: DfEE

Department of Education and Science (1978) *Primary Education in England: A Survey by HM Inspectors of Schools*, London: HMSO

Department of Education and Science (1985a) *Education 8 to 12 in Combined and Middle Schools*, London: HMSO

Department of Education and Science (1985b) *The Curriculum from 5 to 16*, London: HMSO

Dodd, E. (1991) 'Identifying needs in the context of appraisal', in Sullivan, M. (ed.) *Change and Development in the Primary School*, Harlow: Longman

Douglas, J.W.B. (1964) *The Home and the School*, London: MacGibbon and Kee

Doyle, W. (1985) 'Effective secondary classroom practices', in Kyle, M. J. (ed.) *Reaching for Exellence: An Effective Source Book*, Washington D. C.: US Goverment Printing Office.

Draft Framework for Numeracy Years 1–6 (1997), Reading: National Numeracy Project

Dunne, E. and Bennett, Neville (1990) *Talking and Learning in Groups: Activity Based In-service and Pre-service Materials*, London: Routledge

Dyer, W. (1987) *Team Building: Issues and Alternatives*, Harlow: Addison-Wesley

Earley, P. (1994) *School Governing Bodies: Making Progress?* Slough: NFER

Earley, P. and Kinder, K. (1994) *Initiation Rights: Effective Induction Practices for New Teachers*, Slough: NFER

Edmonds, R.R. (1979) 'Effective schools for the urban poor', *Educational Leadership* 37(1): 15–27

Elliott, J. (1991) *Action Research for Educational Change*, Buckingham: Open University Press

Elliott, M. (1988) *Keeping Safe: A Practical Guide to Talking with Children*, London: Hodder and Stoughton

Eraut, M. (1997) 'Developing expertise in school management and teaching', in Kydd, L., Crawford, M. and Riches, C. (eds) *Professional Development for Educational Management*, Buckingham: Open University Press

Forward, B. (1988) *Teaching in the Smaller School*, Cambridge: Cambridge University Press

Fullan, M. (1992) *Successful School Improvement*, Buckingham: Open University Press

Fullan, M. and Stiegelbauer, S. (1991) *The New Meaning of Educational Change*, London: Cassell

Gaine, C. (1987) *No Problem Here: A Practical Approach to Education and 'Race' in White Schools*, London: Hutchinson

Gaine, C. (1995) *Still No Problem Here,* Stoke-on-Trent: Trentham Books

Galton, M. (1989) *Teaching in the Primary School*, London: David Fulton Publishers

Galton, M. (1995) *Crisis in the Primary Classroom*, London: David Fulton Publishers

Galton, M. and Patrick, H. (1990) *Curriculum Provision in the Small Primary School*, London: Routledge

Galton, M. and Simon, B. (1980) *Progress and Performance in the Primary Classroom*, London: Routledge and Kegan Paul

Galton, M. and Williamson, J. (1992) *Group Work in the Primary School*, London: Routledge

Galton, M., Simon, B. and Croll. P. (1980) *Inside the Primary School*, London: Routledge and Kegan Paul

Gipps, C. (1994) 'What we know about effective primary teaching', in Bourne, J. (ed.) *Thinking through Primary Practice*, London: Routledge, in association with the Open University

Gipps, C., Brown, M., McCallum, B. and McAllister, S. (1995) *Intuition or Evidence*, Buckingham: Open University Press

Goldring, E. (1997) 'Educational leadership, environmental and boundary spanning', in Preedy, M., Glatter, R. and Levacic, R. (eds) *Educational Management: Strategy, Quality and Resources*, Buckingham: Open University Press

Great Britain Statutes (1996) *Education Act 1996*, chapter 56, London: HMSO

Hall, D. (1997) 'Professional development portfolios', in Kydd, L., Crawford, M. and Riches, C. (eds) *Professional Development for Educational Management*, Buckingham: Open University Press

Hargreaves, A. (1994) *Changing Teachers, Changing Times: Teachers' Work and Culture in the Postmodern Age*, London: Cassell

Hargreaves, D. and Hopkins, D. (1991) *Development Planning 2: A Practical Guide: Advice to Governors, Headteachers and Teachers*, London: DES

Hargreaves, D. and Hopkins, D. (1993) 'School effectiveness, school improvement and development planning', in Preedy, M. (ed.) *Managing the Effective School*, London: Paul Chapman Publishing.

Hastings, N., Schwieso, J. and Wheldall, K. (1996) 'A place for learning', in Croll, P. and Hastings, N. (eds) *Effective Primary Teaching: Research-based Classroom Strategies*, London: David Fulton Publishing

Holt, A. (1993) 'A governor's perspective', in *Drawing the Lines*, DfE Conference Report

Holt, J. (1984) *How Children Fail*, Harmondsworth: Penguin

Hopkins, D. (1993) *The Role of the External Consultant*, keynote address given at the National Association of Educational Inspectors, Advisers and Consultants Annual Conference, York, 10 September

Hopkins, D., Ainscow, M. and West, M. (1997) 'Making sense of change', in Preedy, M., Glatter, R. and Levacic, R. (eds) *Educational Management: Strategy, Quality and Resources*, Buckingham: Open University Press

Huberman, M. (1992) 'Critical introduction', in Fullan, M. *Successful School Improvement*, Buckingham: Open University Press

James, C. and Phillips, P. (1997) 'The practice of educational marketing in schools', in Preedy, M., Glatter, R. and Levacic, R. (eds) *Educational Management: Strategy, Quality and Resources*, Buckingham: Open University Press

Jencks, S., Smith, M.S., Ackland, H., Bane, M.J., Cohen, B., Grintlis, H., Heynes, B. and Michelson, S. (1972) *Inequality*, New York: Basic Books

Kerwood, B. and Clements, S. (1986) 'A strategy for school-based staff development', in Day, C. and Moore, R. (eds) *Staff Development in the Secondary School*, London: Croom Helm

Keys, W. and Fernandez, C. (1990) *A Survey of School Governing Bodies, Vol. 1*, Slough: NFER

Kydd, L., Crawford, M. and Riches, C. (eds) (1997) *Professional Development for Educational Management*, Buckingham: Open University Press

Kyriacou, C. (1986) *Effective Teaching in Schools*, Oxford: Basil Blackwell

Kyriacou, C. (1991) *Effective Teaching Skills*, Oxford: Basil Blackwell

Lane, J. (1989) 'The play group/nursery', in Cole, M. (ed.) *Education for Equality: Some Guidelines for Good Practice*, London: Routledge

Lang, P. (ed.) (1988) *Thinking about Personal and Social Education in the Primary School*, Oxford: Blackwell

Leigh, A. (1994) 'Change and leadership', in Bennett, Nigel, Glatter, R. and Levacic, R. (eds) *Improving Educational Management through Research and Consultancy*, London: Paul Chapman Publishing

Lewis, J. (1985) 'The theoretical underpinnings of school change strategies', in Reynolds, D. (ed.) *Studying School Effectiveness*, London: The Falmer Press.

Little, J.W. (1986) 'Norms of collegiality and experimentation and workplace conditions of school success', *American Educational Research Journal* 19(3): 325–40

Macbeth, A. (1994) 'Involving parents', in Pollard, A. and Bourne, J. (eds) *Teaching and Learning in the Primary School*, London: Routledge

MacGilchrist, B., Mortimore, P., Savage, J. and Beresford, C. (1995) *Planning Matters: The Impact of Development Planning in Primary Schools*, London: Paul Chapman Publishing

Margerison, C. (1978) *Influencing Organisational Change*, London: Institute of Personnel Management

McGuiness, J. (1988) 'Let's start from the very beginning: primary teachers and PSE', in Lang, P. (ed.) *Thinking about Personal and Social Education in the Primary School*, Oxford: Blackwell

Moore, J.R. (1988) 'Guidelines concerning adult learning', *The Journal of Staff Development* 9(3): 2–5

Morgan, N. and Saxton, J. (1991) *Teaching Questioning and Learning*, London: Routledge

Mortimore, P., Sammons, P., Stoll, L., Lewis, D. and Ecob, R. (1988) *School Matters*, London: Open Books

Munn, P. (ed.) (1993) *Parents and Schools: Customers, Managers or Partners*, London: Routledge

Murgatroyd, S. and Morgan, C. (1992) *Total Quality Management and the School*, Buckingham: Open University Press

Muschamp, Y. (1994) 'Target setting with young children', in Pollard, A. and Bourne, J. (eds) *Teaching and Learning in the Primary School*, London: Routledge

National Commission on Education (1995) *Success against the Odds: Effective Schools in Disadvantaged Areas*, London: Routledge

Needham, J. (1994) 'An approach to personal and social education in the primary school', in Pollard, A. and Bourne, J. (eds) *Teaching and Learning in the Primary School*, London: Routledge

Nias, J., Southworth, G. and Campbell, P. (1992) *Whole School Curriculum Development in the Primary School*, London: The Falmer Press

Nias, J., Southworth, G. and Yeomans, R. (1989) *Staff Relationships in the Primary School*, London: Cassell

Nuttall, D., Goldstein, H., Prosser, R. and Rasbash, J. (1989) 'Differential school effectiveness', *International Journal of Educational Research* 13(7): 769–76

O'Connor, M. (1998) 'The power of feedback', *Times Educational Supplement*, 6 February

Ofsted (1994a) *Improving Schools*, London: HMSO

Ofsted (1994b) *Primary Matters*, London: HMSO

Ofsted (1994/5) *Subjects and Standards: Issues Arising from Ofsted*, London: HMSO

Ofsted (1995) *Planning Improvement: Schools' Post-inspection Plans*, London: HMSO

Ofsted (1997) *From Failure to Success: How Special Measures Are Helping Schools Improve*, London: Ofsted

Olweus, D. (1993) *Bullying at School: What We Know and What We Can Do*, Oxford: Blackwell

Ouston, J, and Maughan, B. (1985) 'Issues in the assessment of school outcomes', in Reynolds, D. (ed.) *Studying School Effectiveness*, London: The Falmer Press

Oxley, H. (1987) *The Principles of Public Relations*, London: Kogan Page

Pinsent, P. (ed.) (1992) *Language, Culture and Young Children*, London: David Fulton Publishers, in association with the Roehampton Institute

Pollard, A. (1985) *The Social World of the Primary School*, London: Holt, Rinehart and Winston

Pollard, A. and Bourne, J. (eds) (1994) *Teaching and Learning in the Primary School*, London: Routledge

Pollard, A. and Tann, S. (1987) *Reflective Teaching in the Primary School*, London: Cassell

Preedy, M. (ed.) (1993) *Managing the Effective School*, London: Paul Chapman Publishing

Preedy, M., Glatter, R. and Levacic, R. (eds) (1997) *Educational Management: Strategy, Quality and Resources*, Buckingham: Open University Press

Pring, R. (1988) 'Personal and social education in the primary school', in Lang, P. (ed.) *Thinking about Personal and Social Education in the Primary School*, Oxford: Blackwell

Purkey, S.C. and Smith, M.S. (1985) 'The district policy implications of the effective school literature', *The Elementary School Journal* 85(3): 353–89

Reynolds, D. (ed.) (1985) *Studying School Effectiveness*, London: The Falmer Press

Reynolds, D. and Cuttance, P. (eds) (1992) *School Effectiveness: Research, Policy and Practice*, London: Cassell

Reynolds, D. and Reid, K. (1985) 'The second stage: towards a reconceptualisation of theory and methodology in school effectiveness research', in Reynolds, D. (ed.) *Studying School Effectiveness*, London: The Falmer Press

Reynolds, J. and Saunders, M. (1987) 'Teacher responses to curriculum policy: beyond the "delivery" metaphor', in Calderhead, M.J. (ed.) *Exploring Teachers' Thinking*, London: Cassell

Reynolds, D., Creemers, B.P.M., Nesselrodt, P.S., Schaffer, E.C., Stringfield, S. and Teddlie, C. (eds) (1994a) *Advances in School Effectiveness Research and Practice*, Oxford: Pergamon Press

Reynolds, D., Teddlie, C., Creemers, B.P.M., Yin Cheong Cheng, Dundas, B., Green, B., Epps, R., Hange, T., Schaffer, E. and Stringfield, S. (1994b) 'School effectiveness research: a review of the international literature', in Reynolds, D., Creemers, B.P.M., Nesselrodt, P.S., Schaffer, E.C., Stringfield, S. and Teddlie, C. (eds) *Advances in School Effectiveness Research and Practice*, Oxford: Pergamon Press

Ribbins, P., Glatter, R., Simkins, T. and Watson, L. (1990) *Developing Educational Leaders*, Harlow: Longmans

Richards, C. (1988) 'Primary education in England: an analysis of some recent issues and developments', in Clarkson, M. (ed.) *Emerging Issues in Primary Education*, London: The Falmer Press

Richardson, T. (1988) 'Education for personal development: a whole school approach', in Lang, P. (ed.) *Thinking about Personal and Social Education in the Primary School*, Oxford: Blackwell

Riddell, S. and Brown, S. (eds) (1991) *School Effectiveness Research: Its Messages for School Improvement*, Edinburgh, Scottish Office Education Department: HMSO

Rogers, G. and Badham, L. (1994) 'Evaluation in the management cycle', in Bennett, Nigel, Glatter, R. and Levacic, R. (eds) *Improving Educational Management through Research and Consultancy*, London: Paul Chapman Publishing

Rolph, S. (1990) *Budgeting and Equipment for Schools*, London: Hobson

Rudduck, J. (1991) *Innovation and Change*, Buckingham: Open University Press

Rutter, M., Maughan, B., Mortimore, P. and Ouston, J. (1979) *Fifteen Thousand Hours: Secondary Schools and Their Effects on Children*, London: Open Books

Sammons, P., Hillman, J. and Mortimore, P. (1995) *Key Characteristics of Effective Schools: A Review of Effectiveness Research*, London: Institute of Education and Ofsted

Sammons, P., Lewis, A., Maclure, M., Riley, J., Bennett, Neville and Pollard, A. (1994) 'Teaching and learning process', in Pollard, A. (ed.) *Look before You Leap? Research Evidence for the Curriculum at Key Stage 2*, London: Tufnell Press

Scheerens, J. (1992) *Effective Schooling: Research, Theory and Practice*, London: Cassell

Select Committee Report (1986) *Achievements in Primary Schools*, London: HMSO

Shipman, M. (1990) *In Search of Learning: A New Approach to School Management*, Oxford: Blackwell

Simon, B. and Willcocks, J. (eds) (1981) *Research and Practice in the Primary Classroom*, London: Routledge and Kegan Paul

Skelton, M., Reeves, G. and Playfoot, D. (1991) *Development Planning in Primary Schools*, Windsor: NFER–Nelson

Sluckin, A. (1981) *Growing up in the Playground: The Social Development of Children*, London: Routledge and Kegan Paul

Sotto, E. (1994) *When Teaching Becomes Learning: A Theory and Practice of Teaching*, London: Cassell

Stoll, L. and Fink, D. (1996) *Changing Our Schools*, Buckingham: Open University Press

Strain, M. (1990) 'Resource management in schools: some conceptual and practical considerations', in Cave, E. and Wilkinson, C. (eds) *Local Management of Schools: Some Practical Issues*, London: Routledge

Sullivan, M. (ed.) (1991) *Supporting Change and Development in the Primary School*, Harlow: Longman

Tabberer, R. (1997) *Samples for School Profiles*, Slough: Education Management Information Exchange, NFER

Tann, C.S. (1981) 'Grouping and group work', in Simon, B. and Willcocks, J. (eds) *Research and Practice in the Primary Classroom*, London: Routledge and Kegan Paul

Tattum, D.P. (1988) 'Social education is interaction', in Lang, P. (ed.) *Thinking about Personal and Social Education in the Primary School*, Oxford: Blackwell

Taverner, D. (1990) *Reading Within and Beyond the Classroom*, Buckingham: Open University Press

Teddlie, C. (1994) 'The integration of classroom and school process data in school effectiveness research', in Reynolds, D., Creemers, B.P.M., Nesselrodt, P., Schaffer, E.C., Stringfield, S. and Teddlie, C. (eds) *Advances in School Effectiveness Research and Practice*, Oxford: Pergamon Press

Thomas, N. (1993) 'Breadth, balance and the National Curriculum', in Campbell, R.J. (ed.) *Breadth and Balance in the Primary Curriculum*, London: The Falmer Press

Thompson, D. and Sharp, S. (1994) *Improving Schools: Establishing and Integrating Whole School Behaviour Policies*, London: David Fulton Publishers

Tizard, B., Blatchford, P., Burke, J., Farquar, C. and Plewis, I. (1988) *Young Children at School in the Inner City*, London: Lawrence Erlbaum Associates

Tomlinson, S. (1993) 'Ethnic minorities: involved partners or problem parents?', in Munn, P. (ed.) *Parents and Schools: Customers, Managers or Partners*, London: Routledge

Tomlinson, S. and Hutchinson, S. (1991) *Bangladeshi Parents and Education in Tower Hamlets*, London: Advisory Centre for Education

Topping, K. and Wolfendale, S. (eds) (1985) *Parental Involvement in Children's Reading*, London: Croom Helm

Van Velsen, W., Miles, M., Eckhom, M., Hameyer, U. and Robin, D. (1985) *Making School Improvement Work*, Leuven, Belgium: ACCO

Webb, R. and Vulliamy, G. (1996) *Roles and Responsibilities in the Primary School: Changing Demands, Changing Practices*, Buckingham: Open University Press

Weindling, D. (1997) 'Strategic planning in schools', in Preedy, M., Glatter, R. and Levacic, R. (eds) *Educational Management: Strategy, Quality and Resources*, Buckingham: Open University Press

Went, D. (1988) 'Sex education in primary and middle schools', in Lang, P. (ed.) *Thinking about Personal and Social Education in the Primary School*, Oxford: Blackwell

West, M. (1994) 'School improvement and staff development: the Thurston development project', in Bradley, H., Conner, C. and Southworth, G. (eds) *Developing Teachers, Developing Schools*, London: David Fulton Publishers, in association with the University of Cambridge Institute of Education

West, M. and Ainscow, M. (1991) *Managing School Development: A Practical Guide*, London: David Fulton Publishers

Wetton, N. and Moon, A. (1988) 'Starting where children are: health education in the primary school', in Lang, P. (ed.) *Thinking about Personal and Social Education in the Primary School*, Oxford: Blackwell

Wheldall, K. and Lam, Y.Y. (1987) 'Rows versus tables II: the effects of two classroom seating arrangements on disruption rate, on-task behaviour and teacher behaviour in three special school classes', *Educational Psychology* 7(4): 303–12

Wheldall, K. and Merrett, F. (1984) *Positive Teaching: The Behavioural Approach*, London: Unwin Educational Books

Wheldall, K., Morris, M., Vaughan, P. and Ng, Y.Y. (1981) 'Rows versus tables: an example of behavioural ecology in two classes of eleven-year-old children', *British Journal of Educational Psychology* 1(2): 27–44

Whitaker, P. (1988a) 'A speculative consideration of primary education and the future', in Lang, P. (ed.) *Thinking about Personal and Social Education in the Primary School*, Oxford: Blackwell

Whitaker, P. (1988b) 'The person-centred teacher', in Lang, P. (ed.) *Thinking about Personal and Social Education in the Primary School*, Oxford: Blackwell

Whitaker, P. (1993) *Managing Change in Schools*, Buckingham: Open University Press

Wideen, M.F. (1987) 'Perspectives on staff development', in Wideen, M.F. and Andrews, I. (eds) *School Development for School Improvement*, London: The Falmer Press

Wideen, M.F. and Andrews, I. (eds) (1987) *School Development for School Improvement,* London: The Falmer Press

Wilson, J., Williams, N. and Sugarman, B. (1967) *Introduction to Moral Education*, London: Penguin

Winkley, D. (1991) 'Consultancy in the primary school', in Sullivan, M. (ed.) *Supporting Change and Development in the Primary School*, Harlow: Longman

Woods, P. (1994) 'Chances of a lifetime. Exceptional educational events', in Bourne, J. (ed.) *Thinking through Primary Practice*, London: Routledge, in association with the Open University

Woods, P. (1995) *Creative Teachers in Primary Schools*, Buckingham: Open University Press

Wragg, E.C. (1984) *Classroom Teaching Skills*, London: Croom Helm/Routledge

Wragg, E.C., Bennett, Neville and Carre, C. (1989) 'Primary teachers and the National Curriculum', *Research Papers in Education* 4: 17–37

INDEX